Development Prospects and Options in the Commonwealth Caribbean

Report of the conference jointly sponsored by the British-North American Research Association and the Overseas Development Institute at Ditchley Park, Oxfordshire, February 20-22 1976

Edited by
Edith Hodgkinson

Overseas Development Institute
London

SBN 0-902594-12-5

The Overseas Development Institute is responsible for determining that this work should be presented to the public, but individual members of the Council are not responsible for statements of fact and expressions of opinion contained herein.

Contents

Introduction and Report on the Conference

Edith Hodgkinson
Overseas Development Institute

In February 1976 a conference on the Commonwealth Caribbean was held at Ditchley Park, Oxfordshire, jointly sponsored by the British North-American Research Association and the Overseas Development Institute. It was chaired by Lord Seebohm, member of the Executive Committee of the British-North American Research Association. Specifically the conference was designed to bring together representatives of the Commonwealth Caribbean and of the traditional bilateral and multilateral donors, to define the current economic problems of the area, to present the area's view on how these should be tackled, and to identify the contribution which the traditional donors could make towards their solution. The discussions made progress towards all three objectives, but the progress was uneven.

The definition of the problem

The analysis of the current situation was presented in the first two session papers, on a regional basis, in the subsequent sectoral papers, and in the informal debate stimulated by them. A distinction was drawn between the long-term structural problems of the economies of the area, and the immediate, short-term difficulties created by higher prices of energy and food since 1972. The two are related, in that the area's ability to deal with these higher prices is constrained by its economic structure.

The countries of the Commonwealth Caribbean have always been closely meshed in with the international economy. Resources of land, labour, and capital have been attracted to the export sector, stimulated by a price structure which undervalued those products produced for domestic consumption. One outstanding consequence has been that export crops account for 95 per cent of the value of agricultural production in these countries. Countries endowed with goods marketable overseas — more accurately the export-oriented sectors — have prospered; other countries less well-endowed — and other sectors — made little perceptible advance.

The Commonwealth Caribbean is a text-book example of economic dualism, but in its case the modern (ie export) sector has not brought in and absorbed the backward, traditional (ie domestic-market oriented) sector, and under present price structures there is no chance that it ever will. Yet the position is not stable, for the export sector is not generating sufficient employment to take up the growth in the labour force. The 1970 census showed that around 30 per cent of the labour force was then seeking work, and in all Commonwealth Caribbean countries unemployment has certainly risen since, even in those recording quite creditable rates of economic growth.

In this situation of entrenched external dependence, which was as great on the import side as on the export, the Commonwealth Caribbean found itself particularly vulnerable to the profound changes in the international economic situation since 1973. Its food import bill rose 80 per cent in 1974, there was very little margin to cut down imports of oil which had quintupled in price, and accelerated inflation in the major supplying countries fed into the economies of the area. At the same time the effect of the recession in the industrialised world has been to reduce its demand for Caribbean goods and services (ie tourism), and one reaction by the metropolitan countries to the associated rising unemployment at home has been stricter controls on immigration — an important safety-valve for the Caribbean's unemployment problem. While the boom in sugar prices in 1974 offered a respite to the producers of this commodity, that respite has proved temporary and — with the exception of Trinidad and Tobago — the Commonwealth Caribbean is facing a critical payments problem. Even the massive rise in the Jamaican government's take from the bauxite industry has now been absorbed. In the more developed countries (MDCS) — Jamaica, Guyana and Barbados — the payments problem is manifested in reduced import capacity. The less developed countries (LDCS) — the Windwards and Leewards — have found themselves unable to meet essential recurrent spending needs. With few resources and backward economies, these countries have always had a slender tax base, but whereas before 1973 the average budget deficit was EC$2m, after it was EC$5m. While none of the countries of the Commonwealth Caribbean could be said to be without its problems, what has happened is that regional dualism — between the MDCs and the LDCs — has been reinforced. For example, while income per head in Trinidad and Tobago — already high for the region — has doubled, that of Grenada — one of the area's lows — has been halved.

This widening disparity must have serious implications for the process of regional economic integration. One reaction, of course, could be to cling together in an increasingly adverse world. The proposal for a regional alumina project — using energy from Trinidad and ore from Jamaica and Guyana — can be seen as such, as also the proposals for regional livestock development[1] and the cement project[2]. At the same time it must be remembered that a regional balance of payments has no operative meaning: individual governments look at their own payments position, and an outward flow is outward whether it goes to another Commonwealth Caribbean country or to the United States. So it was not

---

1 See the paper by K. L. Roache, 'Prospects for Agricultural Growth in the Comonwealth Caribbean for the Next Ten Years'.

2 See the paper by Earle C. Baccus, 'Prospects for Industrial Growth in the Commonwealth Caribbean in the Short and Medium Term'.

surprising when, as part of the overall programme to restrict import spending, the Jamaican authorities in late 1975 brought goods from CARICOM[1] under its quota limits. And liberalisation for CARICOM goods and diversion to that source of imports represents a not easily replaceable loss in tax revenue for all the member countries.

Solutions to the area's problems

This analysis of the problem was broadly accepted at the conference. The need for a solution — and for that solution to spring from the Caribbean itself — was also agreed. But while the existence of a diversity of views within the area was evident, the conference discussions enumerated only two major approaches — the regional and what will be called the alternative. The views of individual governments were not expressed, although their existence — and the likelihood of conflict between them — was implicit throughout the discussions and the papers, most clearly in those on tourism and industry. It was well understood that such national views are the immediately operative ones. Their absence — unavoidable in a small conference without unfairness to one or more — was a regrettable if inevitable feature.

The conference did, however, reach its high points in the authoritative and fluent statement of the regional and alternative views. The former is crystallised in the paper by Alister McIntyre, the latter was expressed in the course of the discussions. The two do not represent opposite poles, but they do propose different lines of approach and would lead to different types of society.

The regional solution essentially seeks to transform the area's economy without overturning the existing institutional structure. It derives from the fact that in a group of countries most of which have a population below 200,000 considerable savings can be achieved through the pooling of services and considerable losses avoided through the complementary development of production activities. Greater co-operation between the different countries of the Commonwealth Caribbean can thus enhance the use of indigenous resources and lessen dependence on imports. The CARICOM Secretariat is engaged in devising proposals along these lines. For example, the livestock development plan aims to cover the area's 1973 import requirements within ten years[2]. But the regional solution is not only about import substitution. An import element is the spreading of benefits from the well-endowed to the less well-endowed — ie from the MDCs to the LDCs. This would lessen the latter's dependence on external sources of capital and thus — as the conference noted —

1 Caribbean Community and Common Market, successor to the Caribbean Free Trade Area (CARIFTA).

2 For details see the papers by Alister McIntyre, 'Possible Response by CARICOM Countries to the Effects of Recent Changes in the International Economic Scene' and by K. L. Roache.

remove some of the pressure on these mini-states to become independent, with all the increase in overhead costs this involves, merely to gain access to international financial bodies such as the IMF. Three moves along these lines were reported in Alister McIntyre's paper[1] — including the agreement to establish a regional financial safety net to provide last-resort financing, with contributions from participating countries and from joint borrowing on international markets.

There are a number of difficulties in the regional solution, and the conference recognised the major ones specifically. The great attraction of the livestock development programme is that no country is required to give up any existing development. It could be argued that this 'attraction' is essential for the proposal's acceptance. Yet since it is only in Belize that the livestock industry is already established, this CARICOM proposal is for the *initiation* of an industry — with all the well-known problems this represents. The LDCs who, at least in the early stages, would receive little in the way of production capacity (and hence employment and income), would need some *quid pro quo* if they were to put up a protective wall against cheaper non-regional sources of supply. The second major problem is that there are some basic problems to which regional co-operation offers no solution. A community of just over 4 million people cannot be self-reliant in many critical areas — its development will still require it to be open to international trade, capital, and technology. Regional co-operation can represent the lessening of external dependence, but it cannot mean its ending — unless the type of development that co-operation is directed towards is very different from that accepted and pursued so far. This is the kernel of the alternative solution. The transformation of the Commonwealth Caribbean economy can be achieved only by a transformation in its structure. Economic activity is to be based on indigenous resources and on indigenous demand, and prices are to be set accordingly. External transactions are to be limited to a small export enclave. With the whole objective one of lessening dependence, those activities which are local input-intensive (such as housing) will be favoured, while those which are not — such as tourism — will be discouraged. This implies a society with political, social and economic attitudes radically different from those now current in the area. The objection was raised at the conference that such a society would not be acceptable to the people of the Commonwealth Caribbean. It was countered with the assertion that the transformation to a self-reliant economy would involve popular participation and thus constitute the mechanism for ideological change.

At this point the absence of the national government was particularly felt — since it is the day-to-day arbiter between these, and other, solutions.

---

1 See page 16.

All the more so at a time when Commonwealth Caribbean governments have shown themselves much more assertive — with Jamaica's introduction of a new tax structure for the bauxite industry and Guyana's take-over of virtually all significant foreign-owned activities. So the conference was left with a situation where no specific objectives were presented to which Commonwealth Caribbean governments, as opposed to individuals, were fully committed.

The donors' role

The conference could consequently give little specific guidance for donors, for it is with individual countries that they must negotiate, and aid to projects or programmes can be effective only if these have the political backing of the recipient. For historical reasons, the traditional donors are not eager to initiate action — even if such were acceptable to the area. Yet any action, or inaction, must influence the situation. So while donors are waiting for the Commonwealth Carribbean to define its objectives, the framework for these objectives is changing. A reduction, or cut-off, in the inflow of external funds would, it is clear, exacerbate the area's payments difficulties, but a further inflow, it was argued by some speakers at the conference, would merely entrench the existing unsatisfactory economic structure.

Such dilemmas for donors are not confined to the Commonwealth Caribbean and it might reasonably be asked what other group of independent/near-independent nations has agreed on the details of their economic transformation. Certainly a two-day conference could not achieve this — and would not be designed to if it were meant to get anywhere.

The conference did come up with one interesting suggestion along lines which national governments have already indicated, by word and deed, that they favour — divestment. The paper by Mike Faber[1] was welcomed at the conference, and was regarded as symptomatic of the sympathetic and co-operative attitude of donor agencies. One proposal, put by the exponent of the 'alternative' solution, was also welcomed, and it is one which fits in with objectives already enunciated and widely accepted in the area — assistance for the re-tooling of the educational system, to develop the local ability to manage and to innovate.

These two proposals exemplify the theme which ran through the conference from its first planning to its final speeches — that whatever form the assistance from external agencies takes, it must be such as to enhance local initiative, for it is up to the Commonwealth Caribbean to deal with its problems. External agencies can help in this and they can hinder: it is for the Commonwealth Caribbean to tell them what its objectives are.

1 'Arguments for Aiding a Programme of Divestment in the Commonwealth Caribbean'.

1. Effects of Recent Changes in the International Economic Scene on the Countries of the Commonwealth Caribbean

Frank Earwaker

Country Programs Division,
Latin America and Caribbean,
World Bank

It is inevitable that a group of small countries such as those of the Commonwealth Caribbean should be highly vulnerable to the vicissitudes of the world economy. Handicapped by small size, economic fragmentation and external dependence, conventional wisdom may lead us to expect that these countries would be dealt a heavy blow by the turbulent events that have beset the world economy in recent years. To some extent this expectation was well founded. The events of the last several years have indeed had profound repercussions in the Caribbean and have necessitated a number of sharp adjustments. Nor is the process of adjustment yet complete. The region is still feeling its way towards a new equilibrium and towards a new relationship with the world at large.

Sufficient time has elapsed, however, to be able to assess some of the changes that have taken place. The total economic disaster that was predicted by so many observers a couple of years ago has not materialised. The economies of the Commonwealth Caribbean have demonstrated a remarkable and unexpected resilience in the face of the world recession. Although there have been many setbacks there have also been substantial gains, so that on balance the region as a whole may be better placed to tackle its fundamental development problems than it was two or three years ago.

The recent development experience of the Commonwealth Caribbean

The changes that have taken place recently can best be appreciated when viewed against the development experience of the Commonwealth Caribbean over the last ten or fifteen years. It is no easy matter to summarise this experience, however, in view of the diversity which exists within the region. Particularly significant in this respect is the dichotomy btween the four more developed countries (MDCs) — Jamaica, Trinidad and Tobago, Barbados, and Guyana — and the other less developed countries (LDCs) — Belize, the Windward Islands and the Leeward Islands. The LDCs have a total population of about 700,000 and they labour under the severe handicap of an extremely poor resource endowment which, combined with the disadvantages of small size and physical isolation, makes it impossible for them to compete with their four larger partners on an equal footing. By way of contrast, the more developed countries with a total population of 4 million account for 94% of the region's GDP and have an average income per head which is almost double the level of $430 estimated for the LDCs in 1972[1]. This higher income level owes much to the systematic development of a resource base which, although narrow, is good by the standards of developing countries as a whole. Petroleum, bauxite, sugar, and tourism figure prominently amongst the foreign exchange earnings of the MDCs, and the high levels of direct foreign investment associated with these sectors have underpinned a long record of economic growth.

The general pattern of development in all four MDCs has been broadly similar in the recent past. The decade of the sixties was a period of steady growth averaging 5% a year and both the central government finances and the balance of payments were sound. During this period there was a tendency for the gap between imports and exports to widen, but this was offset by heavy inflows of foreign investment directed towards the development of mineral resources and tourism. The situation changed in 1972, however, when the flow of foreign investment began to slacken appreciably. In part this was a result of specific sectoral considerations such as the completion of a major expansion of Jamaican bauxite and alumina production capacity. More fundamentally, however, it reflected a deterioration in the general climate of international investment, and this exposed the vulnerability of the MDCs in the face of an adverse trade balance. By the time the several governments had initiated corrective action, the region was in the throes of a foreign exchange crisis which persisted through 1973 and into 1974.

In 1972 there was also a significant change in the pattern of domestic price stability which the region has traditionally enjoyed. Prices had risen at an average annual rate of no more than 3% or 4% during the sixties, but in 1972 all four of the more developed countries experienced an unparalleled inflation which reached levels higher than 30% in 1974 in some countries and which still persists today. There is reason to believe that the initial impetus of inflation came from outside the region, and this serves to underline the external dependence of the Caribbean

1 The conventional grouping of countries into MDCs and LDCs is not without its shortcomings, however. Guyana, with an income per head of $400 in 1972, has some of the characteristics of an LDC. Belize, with an income per head of $670 in 1972, shares some of the characteristics of an MDC.

countries. In the MDCs as a whole, imports amount to nearly 50% of GDP, and such staple commodities as wheat and rice figure prominently in the import bill. The world prices of these basic foodstuffs have risen more than threefold since 1972. In economies other than Trinidad and Tobago, moreover, the increase in petroleum prices also contributed to domestic inflationary pressures.

Barbados provides an excellent illustration of the extent to which the Caribbean economies suffered from imported inflation. An item-by-item review of the retail price index in that country, separating imported goods from domestically produced goods, shows that the former category accounted for 70% of the rise in the index during the twenty-four month period from August 1972 to August 1974.

However, although the initial inflationary impetus was external in origin, it would appear that the effect of this imported inflation was to trigger a series of wage and price reactions which thereby sustained the inflationary spiral. Domestic forces have now assumed a prominent (and perhaps a dominant) role in the continuing inflation. At the root of this problem is a strong tradition of labour unionism which has exacted high wage settlements quite out of line with any increases in productivity. From the present perspective there can be no doubt that the control of inflation in the Commonwealth Caribbean now hinges upon the implementation of an effective incomes policy more than upon any other single factor.

Concurrent with an accelerating inflation and a loss of foreign exchange reserves, all four MDCs experienced a deterioration in their central government finances during 1973. In Jamaica and Trinidad and Tobago central government savings were very low by historical standards, while both Barbados and Guyana had a deficit on current account. There can be no doubt that these budgetary problems reflected difficulties in the balance of payments — the two things being closely related in the Caribbean context. The weak fiscal position obliged all the MDCs to resort to high levels of external borrowing, frequently from the Eurodollar market, in order to finance the public sector investment programme.

The turbulent events which beset the world economy during 1974 came at a time when the MDCs were already experiencing acute difficulties on a number of fronts. Inflationary pressures were well established, and both the balance of payments and the government finances were under pressure. Coming on top of all these problems, there were serious misgivings that the unparalleled rise in energy prices might precipitate a major crisis in all the MDCs other than Trinidad and Tobago, which was obviously in a strong position as a petroleum exporter. So imminent did this danger appear in early 1974 that international financial and development agencies prepared themselves to provide extraordinary financial assistance to the region as an emergency measure, and Trinidad and Tobago made arrangements for the quick disbursement of balance of payments assistance to its partners in CARICOM. It transpired, however, that fears for the financial viability of the Caribbean nations were premature. In the event, Barbados and Guyana were saved from a financial crisis by subsequent developments in the world price for sugar, while Jamaica introduced a levy on the production of bauxite which more than compensated for the increase in its petroleum import bill. The net effect of all these changes has been to improve the terms of trade of the MDCs, and their medium-term balance of payments prospects are correspondingly much better than was envisaged at any time in the past two or three years. This rapid turnabout in the fortunes of the more developed Commonwealth Caribbean countries in the midst of a worldwide economic recession is, perhaps, the most remarkable and surprising development in the economic history of the region.

By way of contrast to the MDCs, the LDCs have never in the past demonstrated independent viability either with respect to their government finances or with respect to their external payments position. A modest 2% to 3% annual increase in production per head during the decade of the sixties was made possible by substantial subventions from the United Kingdom to the public finances, both on current and on capital account. To some extent this has compensated for a negative level of gross domestic savings, but it has not been sufficient to generate a rate of growth comparable to that of the MDCs.

It has been widely reported that the LDCs particularly have suffered from the recession in metropolitan countries and from the escalation of food and energy prices. In many of these countries imports amount to 70% or 80% of GDP so that it can be readily appreciated that world inflation would have a major impact. Imports are financed from three sources, namely agricultural exports, tourism, and financial assistance from abroad. The latter is of particular importance insomuch as all these countries have a negative resource balance which in some cases may be equivalent to as much as 40% or 50% of GDP. Since 1974, however, only agricultural exports have been able to keep pace with the increasing cost of imports. Financial assistance from abroad has been more or less constant in current prices and has therefore diminished in real terms. Earnings from tourism declined seriously as a result of lower incomes and economic uncertainty in metropolitan countries. The net result of all these factors has been a sharp decline in the import capacity of the LDCs. In most countries this would manifest itself in the form of an acute balance of payments crisis, but because of the particular monetary arrangements of the Windward and Leeward Islands a lower capacity to import has been transformed directly into a fall in real incomes.

Towards a more assertive economic policy

Drawing together the threads of the many complex events of the last few years, there emerges a new picture of the Caribbean which differs in many respects from the image of the past. In the first place it appears that the Caribbean nations are taking upon themselves a much more active role in shaping their economic relationships with the rest of the world. 1974 marked a turning point in this respect. In that year the more developed countries of the region were able to achieve significant improvements in their balance of payments and fiscal positions despite the world-wide economic crisis. To some extent this was a matter of luck — the spectacular rise in sugar prices is a case in point — but there were also a number of bold policy innovations on the part of governments. The sugar-producing nations renegotiated their long-term sales contracts in order to benefit from the high prices prevailing on the world market. Guyana and Barbados introduced new taxes on sugar to ensure that a large portion of the windfall gains accrued to the Treasury. Trinidad revised its petroleum tax legislation to cream off most of the gains from high petroleum prices. Jamaica used its leverage as the world's largest exporter of bauxite to increase its revenues from that commodity fivefold. All these initiatives involved a much greater use of economic muscle-power than had been customary. Furthermore, all the initiatives were successful in achieving their objectives with respect to consolidating the public finances and the balance of payments. This is not to say that the financial future of the more developed countries is now secure. There are portents of difficulties to come, particularly for those countries such as Guyana and Barbados which are heavily dependent upon sugar (the price of which has fallen significantly in the last twelve months). It does seem, however, that the experience of the last two years may herald a new era of economic management in which governments assert themselves more positively in the conduct of their external economic relationships.

Another manifestation of this more assertive attitude is apparent in the conduct of governments with respect to multinational corporations. For many years the policy of the MDCs has been to establish a greater degree of national control over the operations of multinational corporations, particularly those operating in the mineral and mineral-related sectors. The world economic recession and the oil crisis have given an added impetus to this process, however. In 1974, for example, Guyana nationalised the mining operations of Reynolds Metal and thereby brought the last remaining private bauxite operation of that country into the public sector. In the same year Jamaica announced that it would seek active public participation in all new investments related to the bauxite/alumina sector, while Trinidad adopted a similar position with respect to the future development of its own petroleum and natural gas resources. These policy measures do not represent a departure from previously established trends to extend the area of public ownership and control, but they do represent an acceleration of this process. It would appear that the world economic crisis of 1974 imparted a greater sense of urgency for action in this respect.

By and large the LDCs have been more passive in their reaction to world-wide recession and inflation than have the MDCs. This undoubtedly reflects their much weaker economic position and their greater dependence upon financial assistance from abroad. Recently, however, there have been a number of proposals to strengthen the East Caribbean Currency Authority with the objective of giving it powers akin to those of a central bank. This move undoubtedly reflects a certain frustration on the part of the LDCs that their monetary system permitted them little leeway for manoeuvre in the recent economic crisis. The proposals to strengthen ECCA would give the LDCs access to conventional instruments of monetary management.

The balance of gains and losses

Taking the region as a whole, it appears that the Commonwealth Caribbean is financially much better off than it was a couple of years ago. Its aggregate foreign exchange reserves and fiscal revenues are much greater than at any time in the past and there are prospects of yet further gains in the future. On the other hand, the overall financial position of the region may be misleading insomuch as it masks wide disparities both between nations and within nations. It is possible that the polarisation of rich and poor may have become more acute as a result of the economic recession and world-wide inflation.

The two nations to gain most from the economic developments of the last two years have been Trinidad and Tobago, and Jamaica. In the case of the former it is estimated that gross national income per head increased from $1,140 in 1973 to $1,730 in 1974 as a result of higher revenues from petroleum. Jamaica's achievements were somewhat more modest but nevertheless significant. In that country the bauxite production levy increased gross national income per head from an estimated $910 in 1973 to $1,180 in 1974. Barbados and Guyana also made significant gains in 1974 from the high price of sugar, although the basis of their increased income is more fragile.

In contrast to the MDCs the income of the LDCs declined significantly in 1974. In the case of Grenada income per head is estimated to have declined by 30% in real terms. The case of Grenada may be exceptional, however, because the civil disorders that accompanied independence in early 1974 wrought havoc on the economy. It appears that the decline in real incomes in the Windward and Leeward Islands as a whole during 1974 may have been nearer 10%.

It is noteworthy that Trinidad and Tobago, recognising the plight of the LDCs, has extended financial assistance to them both directly and through the intermediation of the Caribbean Development Bank. This assistance has undoubtedly ameliorated the short-term problems of the LDCs but it has not, in itself, been sufficient to resolve their longer-term problems which are of a fundamental structural nature. If a serious attempt is to be made to redress the imbalance between the MDCs and the smaller nations of the Commonwealth Caribbean (an imbalance that has been aggravated by the world-wide recession), it will be necessary to devise some mechanism whereby a continuous and dependable flow of assistance can be channelled from the former to the latter. The extent to which this objective can be achieved will be a telling indicator of the sincerity and commitment which underlies the Caribbean integration movement.

A second aspect of the increased polarisation that has taken place as a result of economic recession is the apparently widening gap between income groups within countries. This is attributable in large measure to the uneven performance of economic sectors during the last couple of years. The strong financial position of the mineral and mineral-related industries has enabled organised labour in these sectors to secure very high increases in remuneration. Wage levels in these sectors have always been exceptionally high, moreover, in relation to the rest of the economy so that the recent upward adjustments further entrench their privileged position. Other sectors have fared less well. Tourism and manufacturing industry (particularly manufacturing geared towards export markets) have borne the brunt of the recession in metropolitan countries and have been squeezed by slack demand on the one hand and rising costs on the other. Wages in these industries have frequently not kept pace with the rise in retail prices, and many workers have been laid off. Every country in the region has experienced an increase in the already high level of unemployment. This has been an important factor in widening the gap between income groups in the last two or three years.

In other words, recent economic developments appear to have exacerbated the negative symptoms of a 'dual economy' in which the advanced technology and high productivity of the mineral and mineral-related sectors contrast sharply with the more modest achievements of the rest of the economy. The most challenging issue of economic management in the coming years will be to bridge that gap. In this respect attention must focus upon the distribution throughout the economy of revenues from the mineral sectors so that these revenues may be harnessed to promote a more balanced sectoral growth.

2. Possible Response by CARICOM Countries to the Effects of Recent Changes in the International Economic Scene

Alister McIntyre

Secretary-General,
CARICOM

In considering the manner in which the CARICOM countries have sought to respond to the international economic crisis, I shall be confining myself largely to the responses that have been attempted at the regional and international levels, leaving for others the question of responses that have been taking place at a strictly national level. This choice is dictated largely by the fact that I have been personally involved in certain aspects of regional and international action, and I am therefore in a better position to make a contribution on these subjects.

The situation before the crisis

The international economic crisis merely served to exacerbate an already difficult economic situation in the Caribbean. One of the major features of economic performance in the region has been that the apparently impressive rates of economic growth which were achieved during the 1950s and 1960s were not accompanied by any significant transformation of the economic structure. Accordingly, the region entered the 1970s with a backlog of structural problems, the most important of which was the persistence of high rates of open unemployment and under-employment. The 1970 census indicated that the absolute numbers of unemployed in the region were about 160,000 persons or about 13% of the labour force. Projections done on the basis of the census figures indicated that if the average annual rate of job creation achieved between 1960 and 1970 was merely sustained through this decade, then by 1980 the region could well end up with some half million persons actually seeking work.

This chronic unemployment situation has existed in the face of significant under-utilisation of the region's resources. It has been estimated that between 1960 and 1970 some 500,000 acres of land went out of production in the region at a time when the area was spending the equivalent of 10% of its GNP on imports of food. Some evidence also existed of the under-utilisation of existing capacity in the manufacturing sector, particularly in food processing and the garment industry, while rising imports of consumer goods indicated further scope for import substitution and displacement in this sector.

These deficiencies in the economic structure called for a shift in development strategy that would give greater emphasis to the mobilisation of resources for the satisfaction of regional needs. It was therefore within this context that the regional integration movement was begun with the negotiation of CARIFTA (the Caribbean Free Trade Area) in 1968. From the start, member governments had recognised that the mere freeing of trade, unaccompanied by joint efforts to develop new and complementary lines of production, was unlikely to bring substantial benefits to participating countries. Accordingly, the freeing of trade was seen merely as a first step towards wider arrangements for the integration of production. The institutional framework for developing the latter was provided by the Treaty of Chaguaramas which brought the Caribbean Community — CARICOM — into being in 1973.

The move towards greater self-reliance at the regional level was parallelled by two complementary thrusts at the international level. The first of these involved the development of horizontal ties with other Third World countries. Within the hemisphere growing contacts were developed with the non-English-speaking countries and with the rest of Latin America as those CARICOM countries which had attained independence began to participate in some of the institutions of the inter-American system. At the global level the government of Guyana, with the support of its CARICOM partners, undertook responsibilities for developing a major part of the Action Programme for Economic Cooperation between developing countries which was one of the main results of the Summit of Heads of Government of the Non-Aligned Countries held in Algeria in 1973. It was at that summit that some of the elements of the global crisis began to be recognised and the urgent need for a new international economic order identified.

The second thrust was directed towards changing the pattern of trade and economic relations with metropolitan countries. This involved the negotiation of greater security of access and earnings for traditional exports, wider access for exports of manufactured goods, and improvement in both the volume and quality of resource transfers. These objectives were advanced by the CARICOM countries through their participation in the negotiations which culminated in the Lomé Convention. Like the rest of the signatory developing countries of Africa, the Caribbean and the Pacific (the ACP), the CARICOM countries see the Convention merely as a beginning. In many fields it remains to be demonstarated how far the aspirations recorded there will be transformed into real achievement. Yet the Treaty of Chaguaramas contains many elements that could find their way into a new model of relations between North and South. For instance, STABEX is at least in concept an arrangement that commends itself for global application. By the time of the crisis therefore the CARICOM countries had begun a process at the regional level of shifting towards development strategies with a greater emphasis on self-reliance and structural transformation and on international arrangements which could provide for more active participation in the international economy.

Some elements of the crisis

The first contributor has provided more detail on the precise impact of the crisis on the region and on individual countries. I wish merely to refer to one or two key points. The most important of these is the effect of world-wide inflation. First, it has involved a sharp break with traditional patterns of price increases which could well have lasting effects on economic behaviour. Up to 1972, double-digit inflation was virtually unknown in the region. Since then, retail prices have risen in some years by 30% and more. Inflationary pressure has been particularly severe in Barbados and in the Leeward and Windward Islands because of their exceptionally high dependence on imports. A major element in the inflation has been the spiralling cost of imported food. In nearly every case, food prices rose faster than retail prices as a whole. The escalation of prices was also associated, particularly in 1974, with shortages of certain basic foods and raw maerials. As small buyers in the international market, countries in the region often found that they were far behind in the queue for supplies.

Another component of the crisis, as far as the Caribbean is concerned, was the recession in North America which has directly hit the tourist trade, damaging employment levels and foreign exchange earnings in that sector and seriously affecting the overall level of economic activity, especially in the smaller countries.

Imported inflation and recession in the advanced countries have combined to create unprecedented balance of payments problems for the region. Particularly worrying has been the growth in the import bill for food, rising in one year alone by some 80%, as the value of imports jumped from EC$550m in 1973 to some EC$1 billion in 1974, most of this representing an increase in value rather than volume. However, the balance of payments situation has tended to vary from territory to territory and from year to year. Trinidad and Tobago has been the least affected since in a financial sense at least it received some measure of compensation for the inflation in its import prices through the growth in its foreign exchange receipts from oil. In 1974, the bauxite- and suger-producing countries also experienced a comparatively good year because of new revenue arrangements in the case of the first commodity, and of a temporary upsurge in world market prices in the case of the second. The really bad hit countries were those which did not have a commodity that experienced any temporary upswing. This included most of the

Leeward and Windward Islands which depended on bananas and/or tourism for their export earnings.

By 1975 the temporary relief which the non-oil-producing CARICOM countries had received by way of expanded export earnings had disappeared, while the inflation in import prices continued largely unabated. This has naturally led to a severe deterioration in the balance of payments position of most of the non-oil-exporting countries. The prospects for 1976 are by no means good, and it is not improbable that under certain assumptions the non-oil-producing countries could face a combined balance of payments deficit on current account for this year of the order of EC$1 billion.

In the less developed countries of CARICOM the crisis has shown itself not as a balance of payments problem but as a fiscal problem. Because the LDCs operate Currency Board arrangements, they cannot experience balance of payments difficulties in the sense of having a shortage of foreign exchange. However, an overall deficit in the balance of payments would tend to show itself in a contraction in the rate of economic growth, and in the growth of government revenue. LDCs, like the other countries of the region, had at the same time to face inflationary increases in the cost of supplies for the public sector, as well as wage and salary demands because of the serious inflation. As a result, since 1974 they have been experiencing severe budgetary deficts. It is possible that the combined deficit this year might be anything of the order of EC$20m; and the financing of this is a matter of extreme urgency if basic development and administrative services are to be maintained.

Responses to the crisis at the regional level

Turning to the responses that were made by the CARICOM countries at the regional level, it is useful to distinguish those aimed at the short and medium term from measures directed towards the longer term. As far as the short term and medium term were concerned, the principal aim has been to mobilise additional financial resources for dealing with the balance of payments situation and in the case of the LDCs with the fiscal situation. As far as balance of payments arrangements are concerned, the Heads of Government Conference which met in St Kitts in December last year approved two arrangements, the details of which are now being developed by a technical working party. The first is for the creation of a regional financial safety net that would provide last-resort financing to member countries in balance of payments difficulties. Such a net already exists between the OECD countries and is being proposed for the Latin American countries as a whole. The CARICOM scheme might well be the first to go into operation in the developing world. Careful attention is now being paid to the operational aspects of the scheme since it involves not merely mutual assistance through contributions from the foreign exchange reserves of participating countries, but also joint borrowing on international markets.

The second arrangement is for an expansion of the intra-regional credit facility. Under the present clearing arrangements, each Central Bank and monetary authority extends on a bilateral basis to the others a credit limit of £500,000 with provisions for quarterly settlements in a convertible currency. This means that in theory the maximum credit facilities available under the scheme are £10m or about 10% of the value of intra-regional imports in 1974. The heads of government have agreed that the scheme should be expanded and proposals to this end have already been worked out for ministerial consideration. The intra-regional clearing facility is an important mechanism since it could serve to insulate intra-regional trade from adverse movements in the overall balance of payments situation. Experience with other integration movements has shown a tendency for restrictions to be applied to intra-regional trade whenever member countries experience difficulties with their balance of payments. It is therefore the intention that the CARICOM countries should as far as possible seek to avoid such a situation.

The third financing mechanism which has been used is that of bilateral assistance from countries that have been less seriously affected. In particular Trinidad and Tobago has provided balance of payments support for the three more developed countries of CARICOM and a certain amount of fiscal support to the LDCs. Other CARICOM MDCs have also provided bilateral assistance to some countries. The main effort has however been directed towards the creation of a Special Emergency Fund of EC$40m for the LDCs to which the four CARICOM MDCs have already pledged £5m. It is hoped that contributions from countries with traditional ties with the area will provide the remaining sum needed. The idea is that the fund would be used not merely to provide temporary fiscal support, but also to give initial support to the development of common services among the countries concerned, especially in key areas such as fiscal administration and economic planning.

All the financial measures are essentially designed to buy time until longer-term measures aimed at restructuring the region's economies can take effect. In this connection, CARICOM is now moving into a new phase of integration involving the complementary development of key productive sectors. The primary emphasis is being placed on the domestic agricultural sector in an effort substantially to increase the region's self-sufficiency in food. These efforts are being developed under a scheme known as the Regional Food Plan. Since very little is known about the food plan in this country, I might digress somewhat to say a few words about it.

The idea was agreed upon in 1974 when the governments of the four MDCs decided to set up a working party to prepare specific schemes for increasing food production in the area, with particular reference to animal feeds, meat and dairy products, agro-industrial development, fertiliser requirements, and the establishment of a commercial corporation to undertake agreed developments in the field of agriculture and agro-industry. The working party of officials has gone further and identified a preliminary pipeline of project areas which the Secretariat, along with other regional agencies, is now in the process of elaborating.

The first area to receive specific attention has been animal feeds where two major projects are already well advanced. The first is a corn-soya-black-eye-peas project in Guyana which the governments of Trinidad and Tobago and St Kitts-Nevis-Anguilla are also participating. It involves in the first phase the cultivation of 5,000 acres, perhaps building up over a period of six years to about 12,000 acres. A company was incorporated in November 1975 and has received a loan from the Caribbean Development Bank with the aim that production should start in the course of 1976. The other major project, in which the government of Jamaica is participating, is located in Belize. The output-mix and scale are rather similar to the Guyana project, with an emphasis on corn and soya and with the initial acreage being planned at 7,500, with a possible build-up to some 20,000 acres. One special feature of the project is that it envisages some amount of farmer settlement from Jamaica. A feasibility study which has recently been completed by the Caribbean Development Bank is now under study by the two governments, both of which have indicated a strong interest in the project.

The major emphasis in the technical work this year will be to elaborate a preliminary design for a regional livestock complex which broadly envisages the replacement of the 1973 level of regional imports by a series of complementary projects developed over a ten-year period. The complex envisages total capital requirements of over EC$600m, and will probably yield direct on-farm employment for about 26,000. We are working hard in the Secretariat in co-operation with livestock specialists from other regional agencies and national governments to bring the complex to the feasibility stage by the end of this year, so that concrete action can begin on implementing the various project lines envisaged for individual member countries. Apart from this, we are hoping to take to the pre-feasibility stage some work on a regional programme for fisheries development; and for the development of fruit and vegetable production, including processing, within the LDCs.

As soon as human and other resources allow, we hope to develop a similar sectoral programme for the industrial sector other than agro-industry. Despite the progress which has been recorded with industrial production in the area, it still remains broadly true that regional production is satisfying only about 25% of the regional market for manufactured goods. Indeed, compared with many developing areas of the world, the Caribbean is tending to lag behind in import substitution and displacement with respect to items such as textiles that are typical of the early phase of industrialisation. Needless to say, we have not even begun to exploit the scope which might exist for producing certain basic raw materials that could be critical elements in the development of the manufacturing sector.

Associated with our work on the productive sectors has been the elaboration of plans for improving transportation facilities within the region, particularly in the field of shipping. The heads of government recently gave final endorsement to a five-year investment programme for the West Indies Shipping Corporation which would involve the addition of four new ships to the service. Parallel work is being undertaken on the improvement of port facilities, particularly in areas such as cold storage, and on the improvement of small vessel shipping — which, in the Eastern Caribbean at least, provides important feeder services.

Responses at the international level

Turning to the action being taken by CARICOM countries at the international level to counteract the impact of the international crisis, the efforts so far have been principally directed towards effective participation in the work that is going on for creating a new international economic order. To this end the CARICOM countries have attached great importance to the discussions taking place within the United Nations system, and to the part that they can play as members of the Group of 77 in advancing the cause of the developing countries within fora such as the General Assembly and UNCTAD. In preparation for this participation, the CARICOM group at the Commonwealth Prime Ministers' Conference worked through their spokesman for the establishment of the Group of Experts of which I am privileged to be chairman; and have continued to support the work of the group, as indeed have other Commonwealth governments, in the belief that the achievement of consensus in small groups could contribute towards the building of a wider global consensus. The Caribbean is also providing an input into the Conference on International Economic Co-operation in Paris through the government of Jamaica which is participating in the work of the Commissions for Energy and Development.

At the level of horizontal relations with Third World countries, the past 12 to 18 months have seen an intensification of activity towards the building of new regional and sub-regional institutions for economic co-operation. The CARICOM countries have been participating in the development of the Latin American Economic System (SELA), and were associated with Trinidad and Tobago in sponsoring a resolution at the last session of the Economic Commission for Latin America for the creation of a Caribbean Committee for Development and Co-operation. This latter commitee held its first meeting in Havana in November 1975 and is well on its way with establishing a work programme that could build effective links between the English-speaking and non-English-speaking countries. Finally, the CARICOM countries continue to work with Guyana in advancing the Action Programme for Economic Co-operation in the belief that major possibilities lie ahead for strengthening ties between the Caribbean and other developing areas.

The impact of the international crisis and the region's responses to them yield at least one important conclusion. They underscore the growing importance of regional and international action as compared with national action. The establishment of a just international order requires the creation of a new inter-dependence based on a more balanced distribution of economic power between the developed and developing countries. The creation of sub-regional and regional groupings and the development of inter-regional co-operation represent important possibilities for strengthening the economic position of other developing countries *vis-à-vis* the rest of the world. For most developing countries therefore, development based upon unilateral action within the international community no longer represents a viable alternative. This is particularly the case for the smaller developing countries which individually have very limited bargaining power in relation to larger entities, whether these be governments or corporations.

If this view is correct, then it follows that a major purpose of the new international economic order must be to strengthen regional institutions and to promote regional efforts at development. This proposition is already well accepted in principle, but tends to be honoured more at the level of rhetoric than of concrete action. An important initiative in favour of regional development has been taken in the Lomé Convention where a proportion of the European Development Fund has been set aside for the financing of regional projects. The early implementation of these provisions could serve as an important pilot project, the results of which might be amenable to wider global implementation. It would be important if this conference can extend the search for ways in which the mechanisms of international co-operation can be directed towards support of the regional efforts in the Third World.

3. Prospects for Agricultural Growth in the Commonwealth Caribbean for the Next Ten Years

K. L. Roache

Agricultural Adviser,
Barclays Bank of Jamaica Ltd

A review of the performance of agriculture in the Commonwealth Caribbean suggests that to attempt to speak on prospects for growth is perhaps presumptuous. Insofar as growth implies increase, the record of agriculture in CARICOM has been disappointing. Strangely enough, the prospects for growth have been fairly obvious for some time. It will be the main object of this paper to isolate some of the prospective growth areas and discuss constraints to growth in the view that, growth being a dynamic process, a static situation implies decline.

The international food situation

It has been said that fundamental changes in West Indies agriculture only occur as a result of a crisis. I do not think I need to elaborate on the international food situation to an audience of this calibre. However, in relation to the topic being discussed, a brief comment on certain aspects is perhaps pertinent. Some of you will recall an article in the *New York Times Magazine* of 5 January 1975 written by Wade Green entitled 'Triage, Who shall be fed? Who shall starve?' In this article the author discussed the implications of the advocacy of the unsentimental, morally uncomfortable practice of selecting areas and countries for making the most efficient use of scarce food resources.

In 1973, the world experienced a sharp increase in food prices as a result of diminished levels of world food reserves (largely in the USA). There is some feeling in that country that it should no longer carry a great proportion of the world reserves. It has also been suggested, in certain quarters, that the US food surpluses will be disposed of purely on the strength of two criteria, namely, balance of payments or balance of power — keeping strategically important countries friendly. We are therefore witnesssing the emergence of food and food supply as a major focus of international diplomacy.

The above comments presage a situation in which food supplies to developing countries like CARICOM could be curtailed because of inability to purchase (owing to high prices), unavailability of supplies, or inaccessibility of supply.

In this sort of situation, the Caribbean Community has to re-examine the theory of comparative advantage.

The Caribbean Community food situation

The paradox of the CARICOM situation is the continuing high importation of foodstuffs into a predominantly agricultural region. Recent indications are that the region has shifted from being an agricultural surplus area to a deficit area.

With the exception of Guyana, land in farms occupies 45% of the total land area of the region. The percentage of the working population engaged in agriculture varies between 20% and 50% for the individual territories. The contribution of agriculture to the GDP, according to Brewster and Thomas[1], ranges from 12% to 43% and a high correlation has been observed between the levels of development attained by the various territories and the size of their respective agricultural sectors.

Community imports of food for 1973 were estimated at EC$500m. With increased prices, it is estimated that the food import bill for 1974 will have been double that figure.

The failure of the Community's agricultural sector to respond to an increasing demand for food can be traced to a pattern of specialisation developed over the centuries of colonial rule. The bulk of the agricultural income of the area is derived from sugar and bananas. The structure of the agricultural sector is one of two production entities, namely:

(a) plantation sector, producing primarily export crops on the better farm lands of fairly extensive acreages, relatively well-developed;

(b) domestic food sector, consisting of small peasant farms on marginal lands, largely undeveloped.

Agricultural development in the CARICOM area has been based on specialisation of plantation production involving a narrow range of major crops which are highly dependent on protective trading arrangements. With the growing preference for non-discriminatory trading arrangements, and the high proportion of the region's income spent on imports of agricultural products, rationalisation of agriculture appears to be an appropriate strategy. Herein rationalisation is conceived to be a process which would contribute to some level of national rather than regional specialisation, which should lead to greater regional import substitution.

The rationalisation strategy places great emphasis on shifting rural consumption patterns in favour of locally produced food and on the development of an agricultural sector oriented to satisfying domestic

1 H. Brewster and C. Y. Thomas, *The Dynamics of West Indian Economic Integration,* Institute of Social and Economic Research, University of West Indies, Jamaica, 1967.

consumption as far as is technologically possible. It also features a reassessment of the role of agriculture in:

(a) providing additional opportunities for employment;
(b) supplying primary inputs for agro-based industries;
(c) increasing levels of domestic food production;
(d) reducing the high food import bill and conserving foreign exchange.

This is being treated with urgency at the political level and the development of an action plan is in the preliminary stages of preparation.

In conjunction with the rationalisation of agricultural production, regional co-operation in agricultural marketing is of vital importance. This was recognised from the early days of the Caribbean Free Trade Area (CARIFTA), and the inclusion of an Agricultural Marketing Protocol as an integral part of the CARIFTA Agreement as the major instrument of agricultural policy is proof of this concern. It is interesting to note that the protocol is essentially a marketing agreement and makes no provision for regulating production. Hence the current emphasis on rationalisation.

Regional import substitution

An analysis of the CARICOM import bill reveals a large and vibrant market for livestock products. The region's imports of livestock products for 1973 amounted to EC$173m. Indeed, as early as 1967, Brewster and Thomas[1] isolated livestock as the sector in which the scale and scope for import replacement was considerable, and proceeded to document the benefits that could accrue on the basis of a regional approach to production.

Bearing in mind the high income-elasticities of livestock products, the demand projection for these products within the region in the next five years assumes staggering proportions. The estimated consumption of meat products in recent years is set out in Table 1. These are modest levels. It is estimated that, in terms of protein requirements, consumption is below desired minimum levels for approximately 50% of the population. The livestock sector, therefore, represents an area of major growth potential within CARICOM well suited to a regional approach to production and marketing, wherein national programmes would be complementary.

On the basis of replacing the 1973 import levels for beef and dairy products by 1985, the projected placement of dairy cows is in the order of 170,000 animals. For beef, the estimated increase in the beef herd is 100,000 animals. An estimated 500,000 acres of improved pastures would be required to support the number of animals specified above. Opinions vary with regard to the number of additional jobs created at the primary production stage to achieve these targets. An estimate of 20,000 is perhaps not unreasonable. In addition, new job opportunities

1 *Ibid.*

will be created by the processing industry which will be required to handle the increased production. A study carried out in Jamaica[1] estimated the labour requirements for a meat plant designed for an annual throughput of 49,200 head of cattle and 62,500 pigs to be 150 people. For a dairy processing plant designed to handle 50,000 lb of milk daily, the labour requirement is estimated to be 90 people. With a projected target of 574m lb of fresh milk per annum and a beef target of 50m lb by 1985, the employment opportunities quoted assume major significance (see Table 2).

Self-sufficiency in mutton, pork and lamb in the next ten years, along with the target of beef and milk products previously mentioned, will create demand for fertilisers (see Table 2), animal feeds, and veterinary supplies. With regard to the first two mentioned, there is some scope for local production. Feed requirements vary with the type of production practised; however an annual requirement of 500m lb of corn and 100m

Table 1. Estimated average per caput consumption of meat and meat products in the Commonwealth Caribbean 1960-1967 (lb)

Item	1960	1961	1962	1963	1964	1965	1966	1967
All meats[1]	37.2	37.9	39.49	40.2	44.9	44.7	44.9	47.3
Imported beef and veal[1]	4.1	4.0	4.2	4.8	5.4	4.9	4.5	4.3
Local beef and veal[2]	9.7	10.8	9.9	9.7	9.9	9.5	10.2	9.6
Imported pork products[1]	5.1	5.0	5.0	5.2	5.6	5.2	4.6	4.1
Local pork products[2]	3.8	3.3	3.4	3.3	3.3	3.1	3.3	3.9
Mutton and lamb[3]	2.0	2.1	2.0	2.0	2.0	2.0	1.9	2.2
Poultry meat[4]	6.3	7.3	8.7	9.0	10.7	12.3	13.2	15.7
Other meats[1]	5.9	5.6	6.6	6.2	7.7	7.3	7.1	7.2

Source: J. M. Mayers and H. W. Blades, *Meat Production and Consumption Statistics of the Commonwealth Caribbean,* Department of Agricultural Economics and Farm Management, UWI, St Augustine.

1 Excludes St Vincent 1960, 1961; Montserrat 1966; Grenada 1964, 1967; St Kitts 1962.
2 Excludes St Vincent 1960, 1961; Grenada 1964, 1967.
3 Excludes St Vincent 1960, 1961; Montserrat 1966; St Kitts 1962.
4 Excludes St Vincent 1960, 1961; Montserrat 1966; St Kitts 1962; Belize 1960, 1961, 1962.

lb of soyabean meal appears likely. Additionally, the development of industry based on processing by-products, hides, and offals would offer considerable employment.

1 Personal communication from F. Anderson, 1974.

Financial implications of expansion of the livestock sector

Jamaican workers[1] report a capital investment of EC$1,400 per acre for dairy enterprises. Land price was averaged at EC$500 per acre and livestock costs accounted for 32% of total investment cost. The comparable figure for a beef grazing and fattening enterprise is EC$958. Admittedly costs in Jamaica tend to be higher than the average levels in the Community; nevertheless, since these costs applied to 1973, it is possible that, with inflation, they are relevant to present costing within the area. At the targeted levels of production, capital investment, using Jamaican costing, would be EC$44m for dairy and EC$17m for beef. These figures relate only to establishment costs. The estimates in Table 2 cover other capital costs (infrastructure, processing facilities etc) and indicate the major financial implications of expansion of the whole livestock sector to meet 1973 import demand.

Growth constraints

Mention was made previously of the identification of the livestock sector as an area of priority insofar as regional production and co-operation were concerned. The question could well be asked as to the reason for inactivity in this sector during recent years. McIntosh[2] maintains that the most crucial constraints to livestock development in the community are:

(1) the lack of extensive, highly productive land resources for livestock production (Guyana and Belize possibly excepted);

(2) the low livestock population with a generally low food conversion efficiency.

Ayre-Smith[3] makes a distinction between the producers' objectives and national objectives in increasing the efficiency of beef production. He further states that the removal of impediments, the provision of services, and the use of innovations are all processes necessary for improving beef production efficiency. Impediments in the CARICOM Region include price control, land tenure and marketing.

Impediments

Price control

The downfall of the CARICOM livestock producer has been the system of price control. Governments of the region have instituted price controls on several meat and dairy products using arbitrary methods. The experience in some parts of the Caribbean has been that beef prices have been fixed too low for commercial producers to make a profit, with little or no

1 K. B. Davidson, Agricultural Division Report, Alcan Jamaica Ltd, 1973.
2 C. E. McIntosh, 'Production Implications of Market Practices in the Caribbean Livestock Sector', Regional Livestock Meeting, Trinidad, 1975.
3 R. A. Ayre-Smith, 'Increasing the Efficiency of Beef Production in Developing Countries,' Conference on Beef Cattle Production in Developing Countries, University of Edinburgh, 1974.

Table 2. Estimated requirements for capital, land, labour and fertilisers of CARICOM livestock self-sufficiency programme

Project	Total capital investment	Land	Farm employment	Fertilisers	
				Sulphate of ammonia	Mixed
	EC$m	'000 acres	'000	'000 tons	'000 tons
Dairy and dairy products	482[1]	317	13	48	16
Beef and beef products	89[2]	160	1	24	8
Mutton and lamb	43[3]	49	2	7	2
Hatching eggs	6[4]	—	0.6	—	—
Livestock feeds (acreage equivalents)	286[5]	329	7	190	96
Total	906	855	23.6	269	122

1 Assuming EC$3,201 investment per breeding animal. Based on ' A Study to Determine the Feasibility of Supplying Guyana with Dairy Products'—Experience Incorporated.
2 Assuming EC$1,117 investment per breeding animal.
3 Assuming EC$338 investment per breeding animal.
4 Assuming EC$16 investment per breeding animal.
5 Based on the Feasibility Study for the Production and Marketing of Corn/Soya Bean in the Intermediate Savannahs of Guyana.
Source: CARICOM Secretariat.

differentiation between prices of the various portions of the carcass. As Ayre-Smith[1] has pointed out, in 1973 several countries controlled the retail price of domestically produced beef at approximately $1.00 per kilogram for all portions of the carcass, despite the fact that studies undertaken by the Caribbean Development Bank indicated that retail prices of $1.40 to $4.50 per kilogram, according to carcass portion, were necessary to allow reasonable profit from fully-costed commercial beef production enterprises. During the same period, imported frozen beef retailed between $2.00 and $6.00 per kilogram. It is of interest to note that imported beef is not subject to price control, and is usually sold at a maximum percentage above landed cost at the wholesale level of 10% to 15%, and a further 15% to 20% above wholesale price at the retail level.

The fixing of prices for locally-produced food at low, usually unremunerative, levels arises out of the propensity of our political leaders

1 *Ibid.*

to believe that domestic agriculture should function as a provider of cheap food for the population. This attitude is perhaps the single most important deterrent to livestock expansion in the CARICOM area. The price control system is a disincentive to improving quality and quantity of produce. Imposing import restrictions does not lead to increased domestic production as long as restrictive price control measures prevail. The short-term policy of low prices, advocated on nutritional grounds, is defeated in the long run as nutrition of the population suffers through lack of development of the sector. Besides, the evidence indicates that imports of meat at prices considerably in excess of domestic controlled prices are a constant and regular feature of even the less developed countries of the Community.

Land tenure

The uneven distribution of land, wherein farms of less than five acres account for 70% of the total number of farms of the region, and at the other end of the scale, farms of 100 acres or more comprise 1% of the number and 47% of the total acreage, presents a formidable problem with regard to changing production patterns. It must be remembered that, historically, the larger farms have produced export crops, and diversification, whilst accepted as a national course, has not been enthusiastically implemented for various reasons, one of these being the existence of linkages as a primary producer to a foreign-owned manufacturing entity.

Marketing system

Although the existence of a buoyant market for livestock products has been identified, much remains to be achieved in terms of institutional arrangements for moving products to the market place. Efficient beef production involves proper presentation to the consumer and optimal use of offal. There is a shortage of adequate processing facilities in the region for beef, pork, and to a lesser extent milk. The features of the markets for imported meat and poultry which have implications for the development of the livestock industry in the region have been described by McIntosh[1] as follows:

> 'The significant structural feature of the markets for imported products is that there is a high degree of concentration diminishing from the importer/wholesaler to the retailers, whereas the locally produced product is characterised by its low concentration throughout the channels of distribution. (In the poultry industry there is a tendency towards high concentration in the processor-distributor segment.) The markets for locally produced products would normally be determined more by supply and demand whereas the prices of

---

1 McIntosh, *op. cit.*

imported products are administered. The markets for local products are low in volume in relation to the number of firms as opposed to the high volume controlled by few firms on the import side. It is not surprising therefore, as the data for Trinidad and Tobago suggest, that the market margins for locally produced beef tend to be higher than those for imported beef. The implication is that the marketing system for beef places the producers of local beef at a disadvantage *vis-à-vis* foreign suppliers. On the question of market conduct, the high concentration of firms in the import sector allows not only price administration but supply control. Quantities are imported that would put an upward pressure on prices.

Although meat storage facilities are available within the Region, most of it is devoted to imported meats. The meat processing industry is also largely dependent on imported supplies. Inadequate slaughtering and storage facilities leave the butcher dealing in locally produced meat little alternative than to take to the market limited supplies. This volume restriction has serious repercussions at the production end. The lack of grading, sophisticated cutting of meat, and proper display restrict market demand and deprive the marketers and producers of valuable income.'

Financial constraints

Innovations to improve efficiency require managerial and enterpreneurial skills. These skills will not be available to financially marginal exercises. Additionally, most innovations have to be financed. Sargeant and Harricharan[1] presented data which demonstrated marginal rates of return for beef and pig production models. In the case of the beef production model land was valued at $50 per acre. This is an unrealistic price. These workers also analysed returns from poultry meat production and concluded that this was a profitable exercise, but cautioned against over-production. The serious constraint on revenue imposed by the price control system was emphasised as well as the detrimental effect of the inefficient application of technology. Personal experience in Jamaica isolates milk production as a profitable exercise attractive to the potential investor.

Other growth prospects

So far, this presentation has been restricted to the growth prospects within the livestock industry. The existence of opportunities for growth in such fields as vegetables and fruit processing is recognised. However, for any significant expansion in these industries to occur, an export market

---

1 V. A. L. Sargeant and H. Harricharan, 'Financial Constraints to Livestock Development in the W. I. Region,' Regional Livestock Meeting, Trinidad, 1975.

is a necessity. The present position, insofar as these products are concerned, is that the volume of supply is not of the order of magnitude to interest actively recognised commodity dealers on a continuing basis. The practice has been for each territory in CARICOM to market such products as it has under its own brand name, and cases of one territory being played off against another territory by an importer have been known to occur. What appears to be necessary is the adoption of a Caribbean brand associated with certain quality standards through which a sufficient volume would be channelled to make an impact on the export market.

There are also possibilities in regard to increased production of rice to replace cereals imports and the conversion of items currently produced to new products. The impact of these projects is small when compared with the magnitude of the import replacement which, as stated previously, a viable and expanding livestock sector could achieve. The aspect of complementarity associated with the development of the livestock sector is an important consideration in an atmosphere of regional co-operation.

The future

Eight years ago, expansion of the livestock sector was identified as the main activity on which functional agricultural integration of the Commonwealth Caribbean should centre. Today, the Caribbean Community is a reality. Unfortunately, the regional approach to livestock expansion is still in its infancy. In the interim, livestock production in the respective territories is at best static. Some of the major constraints have been discussed. In essence, their removal revolves around changes in attitude and government policy.

The present position of the Community with regard to imports of high protein food has forcibly re-emphasised the extreme urgency of initiating expansion. The tragedy of inaction on a regional basis since 1967 and the staggering effects of further inaction at the present time presage a situation in which maximum effort at the political, technical, and financial level is crucial. The hope is that the lesson has been learnt and the desire to survive will precipitate the necessary impetus.

4. Prospects for Industrial Growth in the Commonwealth Caribbean in the Short and Medium Term

Earle C. Baccus
Business Promoters and Consultants Ltd,
Trinidad

History of industrial development in the region

Industrial development in the region had been measured before the mid-50s in terms of the performance of the sugar, alcohol, petroleum, and bauxite and alumina industries in the territories of Barbados, Guyana, Jamaica and Trinidad and Tobago.

These territories were mere primary producers and processors and exporters of indigenous material, and individual growth was measured mainly in terms of the foreign exchange earned through exports of these commodities. The output from these operations in certain territories doubled during the decade 1950-1960.

With the turn of the last decade, a number of member territories, upon gaining their independence, embarked upon vigorous programmes to develop and diversify their economies and pursued a policy of import substitution based on satisfying local demand for goods and services hitherto purchased from the industrialised metropolitan countries. Certain basic industries and operations were established to cater to the increasing demand in the consumption, construction, and services sectors. Cement and building bricks, fertiliser, glass bottles, paints, furniture, and tyre recapping and retreading are but some of the few industries which were established to cater to the demand of growing local populations.

In many cases though, because of a lack of standardisation in consumption, the import substitution effort never brought local supply to more than 50% of domestic consumption.

Despite these early initiatives, primary processing of local materials for export continued to dominate activity in the industrial sector in the region with very little, if any, forward linking to the development of intermediate and final demand products and other sectors of the economy. What had actually happened was the further development of the consumer end-products industry with the establishment of screw-driver-type labour-intensive assembly operations producing refrigerators, stoves, motor vehicles, radios, garments, etc.

Other features of the unbalanced nature of historical industrial growth were the low level of skills developed among the working populace, the dominance of foreign investment and foreign technology, and the low level of re-investment of capital in areas where it was sorely needed for developing and diversifying the sector and the economy as a whole.

The programme of import substitution to some extent accelerated industrial growth but was limited in that it was based on simple replacement and displacement of finished or consumer-oriented goods and services, with heavy dependence on imports of raw materials and intermediates. This structure of production of goods and services was insular in its very nature, geared towards satisfying local demand with no impact on the development of other sectors of the economy such as agriculture or on stimulating exports to regional and extra-regional markets. Growth in the manufacturing sector, however, varied between 12% p.a. in Trinidad and Tobago and 2% p.a. in Barbados. Again it must be remembered that only those territories which gained their independence and hence sovereignity were the ones which pursued this policy of import substitution and therefore experienced growth in the manufacturing sector. The other territories continued to be totally dependent on imports of goods and services from abroad and during this period experienced little or no growth or development in this sector.

With the coming into being of CARIFTA in 1968, it was thought that this institution would foster, and in the case of the non-independent territories provide the framework for, industrial growth in the region. CARIFTA did allow and promote the development of *trade* in the region but it was recognised that expansion of trade, though a necessity, was not a sufficient condition for overall industrial development in the region. The very aspects of the Association Agreement perpetuated the development of light manufacturing consumer-oriented goods of the 'finishing touch' type, again with heavy dependence on imported inputs, technology and investment.

Also, while manufacturing output grew in the independent territories, no growth was reflected in the smaller territories since they became members of CARIFTA with no substantial market nor industrial activity. They therefore were not trading internally nor had they anything to trade with the rest of the region. Furthermore, there was not (nor is there now) in these territories any established raw material base, be it mineral or agro-industrial, so that even simple production and exports of primary material could not be effected.

The coming into being of CARICOM, an increasing awareness of the potential for the development of the raw material base in the various territories and of the need for diversifying the structure of production, coupled with activities and leads undertaken on the international scene, have provided within the past few years the impetus for accelerating industrial activity in the region. The policies or programmes which are being followed by the various territories is adequately summarised in

Article 46 of the Treaty of Chaguaramas which states that the CARICOM countries will 'undertake to promote a process of industrial development through programming aimed at achieving the following objectives:

(a) the greater utilisation of raw materials of the Common Market;

(b) the creation of production linkages both within and between the national economies of the Common Market;

(c) to minimise production differentiation and achieve economies of large-scale production, consistent with the limitations of market size;

(d) the encouragement of greater efficiency in industrial production;

(e) the promotion of exports to markets both with, and outside of the Common Market;

(f) an equitable distribution of the benefits of industrialisation paying particular attention to the need to locate more industries in the Less Developed Countries.'

It is reasonable to conclude that at the end of the last decade and even into the 70s the industrial development programme of the Commonwealth Caribbean territories had not achieved these objectives. It would also be true to say that this programme for industrial development has begun to, and will, provide the basis for present and future industrial growth in the region. Analysis of these provisions and of prospects for the future, based on these provisions, is the subject of discussion in the following section.

Analysis of the programme for promoting industrial growth in CARICOM

The greater utilisation of raw materials of the Common Market

As was previously mentioned, the territories in the region endowed with raw material resources, be they mineral or agriculture-based, have traditionally been exporters of primary processed material in the form of raw sugar, molasses, petroleum, petroleum products, bauxite, alumina, asphalt, animal hides and skins, etc. At one and the same time, these territories have been inefficient users of indigenous materials in that valuable by-products were either dumped at unreasonably low prices or disposed of by processors in the region. Animal hides and skins, natural gas, and bagasse are but a few of the by-products of primary processing in which a greater and more efficient utilisation of these materials could be effected. This would not only have the effect of adding value to domestic production and therefore earning or saving foreign exchange, but would also introduce new technology and much needed skills and assist in the diversification of the sector and promote a more equitable distribution of income in member territories.

Examples of greater and more efficient utilisation of indigenous materials would be the processing of petroleum into petrochemicals, bagasse into fibre-board or furfural, and animal hides and skins into leather and leather products.

It should well be appreciated that development or greater utilisation of raw materials in the area would, in the case of minerals, call for the adoption of technology not now available in the region and capital investments beyond the combined resources of all the territories. The smallness of the regional market would also necessitate extra-regional or international marketing with the attendant need for taking advantage of international, trading bloc or preferential arrangements.

The capital intensity and the nature of the technologies utilised in this development would not in the short and medium term substantially increase employment but would in this time period require highly skilled and professional personnel, at present in short supply in all territories in the region.

These features do not apply to the agro-industrial and manufacturing industries. They are much less capital-intensive, with technological processes which are fairly easily available. These would have a greater effect in diversifying the industrial sector and absorbing the easily trained unskilled and semi-skilled surplus labour that exists throughout the region.

The creation of production linkages

Territories in the region have traditionally not established operations or facilities based on this objective, except in a few isolated cases; eg cotton grown in Carriacou was processed into fibre, yarn, fabric, and finally garments in Trinidad and Tobago. But the creation of production linkages in the area is desirable since production potential is scattered among the territories with no single territory being in a position to undertake fully the exploitation of its individual resources, It also stimulates the development of resources not at present fully utilised. This objective also benefits the Common Market as a whole even if the distribution of the location of industrialisation is not equitable.

At the national level, inter-sectoral development, as say between the agriculture and manufacturing sector for food processing operations and activities, is presently being undertaken in the territories of Belize, Jamaica and Guyana. At the regional level the utilisation of natural gas produced in Trinidad and Tobago to smelt alumina produced in Guyana and/or Jamaica is one example of linking production between economies to effect industrial growth. The production of garments in the LDCs from polyester/cotton fabric woven in Jamaica, which in turn was produced from cotton grown in Belize or Guyana and polyester fibre manufactured in Trinidad and Tobago, is yet another real example of areas where production linkages would assist or encourage an equitable distribution of the benefits of regional industrial development and growth.

Minimisation of production differentiation

Member territories in the pursuit of their individual industrial development programmes embarked upon a course of multiplication of production facilities consistent with satisfying their individual territorial market demand. Import substitution policies also encouraged the proliferation of numerous differing but equally functional models and types of goods and services. These policies had the effect — based on this fragmentation of the markets — of high-cost production, lower levels of output and excessive quality differentiation. The most blatant case in point is that of the motor vehicle assembly industry in Trinidad and Tobago where 32 models of motor cars are being produced for a market of 1m people.

The restriction and standardisation of product types will increase local production runs and thereby generate increased efficiency and economies of scale. In turn, these will reduce costs and provide the avenue for deepening the manufacturing process and backward linkages with other sectors in the economy.

Export promotion to markets both within and outside CARICOM

Apart from the traditional exports of primary processed raw materials, territories in the area have not pursued vigorously any policy of exploitation of extra-regional markets. The policy of import substitution encouraged this dependence of member territories in satisfying and exploiting local demand only.

With the advent of CARIFTA and CARICOM, however, and trade liberalisation measures in these agreements, intra-regional trade in manufactured products increased substantially, from TT$110m in 1968 to some TT$520m in 1974. Despite this growth, regional supply is very far from meeting regional demand, which is estimated at TT$2.3 billion. It will be necessary to shift from domestic import substitution to that on a regional basis in order to exploit this market potential. While, with the coming into force of the Lomé Convention and the US Trade Act and development in the use of regional materials and resources, increasing attention will be paid to the development and exploitation of extra-regional market potential.

An equitable distribution of benefits

There can be no doubt that balanced industrial growth as between and among the territories in the area is necessary for fostering economic integration in the region. Previous efforts at industrialisation led to polarisation towards the territories endowed with natural resources to the disadvantage of those territories without.

Special measures and institutions have been established to remove this imbalance and to create the basis for increased growth in the latter territories. Measures so far have taken the form of the harmonisation of fiscal incentives to industry, Common Market origin criteria, co-operation in the establishment of MDC/LDC joint ventures in the LDCs, and institutions such as the Caribbean Investment Corporation and Caribbean Development Bank. These have gone a long way and will continue to facilitate the establishment of industry and growth in the LDCs.

Already, over twenty subsidiaries of parent companies in the MDCs have been, and are being, established in the LDCs and plans are being elaborated for the establishment there of 35 other ventures which have been identified as feasible undertakings.

Apart from these, there are the spin-off operations from the industrial complexes being established in the larger, resource-endowed territories which, within the context of the special provisions of the CARICOM Treaty, could be more suitably established in the LDCs.

Prospects for industrial growth in CARICOM

In the short and medium term, and certainly in the longer term, a co-ordinated approach to industrial development planning at both the national and regional levels holds the key to prospective industrial growth in CARICOM. At the national level, there has been the distinct tendency to push ahead industrial projects at a pace much faster than agro-industrial projects. These industrial projects were promoted on a project-by-project basis without thorough regard to their impact on other sectors, causing bottlenecks within the economies of member states.

It is heartening to know that most member states have recognised this need and that territories such as Guyana, Jamaica, and St Lucia have formulated and embarked upon this co-ordinated approach to industrial development as part of their overall plan for economic development.

At the regional level, efforts are being and have been made in this direction through programmes and approaches at the level of meetings of national planning agencies, industrial and agricultural planners, and inter-governmental committees and agencies. What is sorely needed, however, is the formulation of an industrial programme for the short and medium term, developed as part of a comprehensive regional development programme and not the *ad hoc* programmes which (though serving and having served useful purposes) have been developed from time to time out of political necessity and as a result of international economic forces.

Specifically, there are a number of goods whose manufacture, based on the structure of regional consumption and resource potential, could form the basis for industrial growth in the region. These are: textile fibre and fabrics; iron and steel; plastics; paper; rubber; industrial chemicals; aluminium; cement; leather and leather products; and glass.

One would therefore expect that efforts at accelerating growth and promoting development potential in industry in the region would be oriented towards the establishment of the manufacture of these commodities for regional consumption and export.

I will now detail specific measures and activities which could lead to increased industrial growth in the short and then the medium term.

Short-term industrial growth prospects

Short-term (two to three years) industrial growth prospects would have to be based on the development of activities and promotion of and implementation of measures and programmes which are ongoing or are already being developed.

In the agro-industrial or food processing sectors, there appears little prospect in the short term for accelerated growth, since this would have to be based on the formulation and implementation of agricultural programmes and the development of regional/local projects and activities which would provide the inputs to the industry. Development or growth in the sector in the short term would therefore be very limited, as the forecast is towards the expansion of facilities to which indigenous agriculture had not been geared in the first place, and materials therefore would continue to be imported in as high a proportion (over 70%) as they are at present.

In the manufacturing sector, growth prospects would occur in the development and expansion of existing production facilities to cater to the market opportunities opened up by the Lomé Convention, the US Trade Act of 1975, and other recently concluded trading and co-operation arrangements with developed countries and trading blocs. It has been estimated, for example, that should full advantage be taken of he provisions in the Lomé Convention, manufacturing output in the CARICOM could increase 100% over the next two years with attendant increases in employment. It has also been estimated that, apart from specific aid received under Lomé, capital investment required for this increase in output would not be of significance since many, if not most, of the manufacturing industries in the region affected already have the necessary production capacity.

In the mining and quarrying sectors, increasing activity in domestic, industrial and public construction will stimulate the demand for products such as cement, limestone, aggregate, sand, clays, and, to some extent, asphalt. Already there are plans afoot in Barbados, Jamaica, and Trinidad and Tobago to increase domestic and regional capacity of cement within the next two to three years. Taken together, the total expansion calls for the provision of an additional 1,000,000 metric tons of cement capacity with additional employment of around 800 people and investment of TT$120m. Equivalent investments and capacity increases would be evidenced in aggregate, stone and clay production facilities throughout the region.

One area of activity which will demand attention over the next two to three years would be the building components sub-sector. Already there are facilities which are being developed for the production of reinforcing rods and bars, structural, roofing and sheeting materials, bricks and tiles, and building furniture. With sustained and dynamic growth in building construction, hardware items would be demanded in increasing quantities.

The next two or three years would see the development of the textile and garment industries with the establishment of cotton and polyester/cotton mill operations in Guyana and Jamaica. Increased regional production of medium-staple cotton in Guyana over the period, and the planned establishment of a polyester fibre and fabric plant in Trinidad and Tobago, would add to the development and creation of a textile industry base which in the long term would provide for self-sufficiency in the region.

In Trinidad and Tobago, increased exploratory and developmental activity in offshore oil drilling would bring increased oil and gas production with concomitant heavy capital and technological inflows. This increased activity would raise the demand for skilled personnel, placing additional pressure on existing manpower development facilities and making their expansion essential.

The medium term

For the medium term, the objectives are mainly increased utilisation of regional raw materials and the forging of backward and forward linkages within the industrial sector and with the rest of the economies as a whole. The medium term would also see the development of extra-regional exports of manufactured goods and increased production linkages between the economies of the member states.

Maximising the use of regional raw materials

Industrial growth based on this objective will see the implementation of agricultural policies to increase the proportion of local/regional materials in the food processing sector.

Regional planning and co-ordination in the agro-industrial sub-sector through the institutions of the Regional Food Plan and Food Corporation would in the medium term also foster the development of fertiliser and pesticide industries. Specifically, the plan envisages in the medium term:

(1) the production of corn and soya beans in Belize and Guyana,
(2) the production, purchase and marketing of agricultural chemicals including fertilisers,
(3) the undertaking of dairying and production of dairy products in Guyana,
(4) the catching, processing and marketing of fish in the region,
(5) the development of a livestock complex centred on the production of meat and meat products.

To implement this plan a Food Corporation has been established with the prime objective of ensuring that the necessary resources (capital, technological, infrastructural, and human) are available.

The development and diversification of the petroleum processing industry is another area in which industrial growth will be stimulated through maximising the use of regional materials. The petroleum industry in the region has been based on the production and primary processing of oil and gas, with raw and intermediate materials exported to extra-regional sources. The plan of Trinidad and Tobago to establish a petro-chemical complex takes on added significance, in that it not only develops the petroleum industry from its narrow base, but provides forward link-ages with many other sectors of the economy through the production of materials for the manufacture of plastics, rubbers, fibres, and detergents.

The capital intensity of the undertaking (TT$12 billion investment for the creation of 1,000 jobs) is balanced by the other medium- and longer-term benefits the project would generate for the economies of the region. Apart from the foreign exchange earned (since a very large proportion of the output would be sold on the international market) the project would stimulate the development of a number of small-scale consumer-oriented operations which would generate employment and income in non-oil sectors of the region's economies, eg textiles, shoes, construction, food packaging, transport, and agriculture. Although plans have been announced for the establishment of a similar complex in Jamaica, based on imported raw materials, it is envisaged that a rationalisation of the production output of the two complexes would be achieved.

The establishment of a sheet glass operation in Guyana catering to the needs of CARICOM is yet another example of the maximisation of the use of regional materials and the expressed desire to achieve economies of scale and rationalisation of production in the region. This operation, which will be based on the processing of indigenous silica sand, it was agreed at official level in CARICOM, would be promoted in Guyana only, and steps have been taken to ensure non-duplication in other member states.

Overall, steps are being taken at the regional level to ensure the maxi-mum use of regional materials in production. The Process List which is to be introduced later this year and the review of criteria for the grant of fiscal incentives to industry would be designed to ensure maximising the use of regional materials and deepening the process of manufacture in the region. As a result of the different stages attained by the developing economies of the member states of CARICOM, the award of fiscal incentives will be approached at two levels. The first will be to integrate existing industries with agriculture and mining, where possible, and encourage these industries to search for extra-regional markets. The industries which cannot be integrated will have to be rationalised in terms of standards and location. The second will be to make it mandatory that new activity that is granted incentives adheres to these new requirements.

Another effort aimed at maximising the use of regional raw materials and by-products is to be found in the establishment of a plant in Guyana for the processing of bagasse and/or tropical hardwoods into pulp and paper. A project of this nature would engender the growth of the paper and packaging industries in the region, and where these are already well established, as for example in Jamaica, Trinidad and Tobago, and St Lucia, provide a backward linkage to these operations. Regional market demand would support a reasonably sized paper-from-pulp operation while at the same time having export potential.

Creation of production linkages within and across CARICOM economies
The promotion of production linkages within the various economies of the region has already been touched on when we considered the prospects for the increased utilisation of indigenous materials in manufacturing. The existence in Guyana and Jamaica of bauxite ores and in Trinidad and Tobago of natural gas provides the basis for the smelting of alumina in the region.

Work has already begun towards the establishment of such an operation in Trinidad and Tobago with the equity participation of the three territories. An investigation has been undertaken on the establishment of a plant costing TT$700m to produce over 200,000 metric tons a year of aluminium in Trinidad and Tobago, which would introduce new technology in the region and generate new and different skills. The project would also involve linkages with other sectors of the various economies and provide substantial indirect employment and manufacturing opportunities.

Another project which would foster the linking of production facilities in the region is the development of the textile and garment industries. The garment and finished fabric industries possess great potential for backward linkages. Mention has already been made of the plans for the provision and development of these linkages aimed at the achievement of self-sufficiency in the region in the long term. It is estimated that within the context of the plans for achieving this goal, direct employment from cotton-growing in Guyana and Belize through fabric-manufacture in Guyana and Jamaica, and increased activity in garment and other textile product manufacture in the MDCs and LDCs would be created for over 8,000 skilled, semi-skilled and unskilled workers. Investment in technology, a small proportion of which would be new to the region, would total some TT$100m. The cumulative treatment criterion would be met by products of these regional operations and they would therefore qualify for preferential entry into the markets of Europe and the USA.

5. Prospects for Tourism for the Next Five Years

Timothy S. S. Prime
Director of Research and Statistics,
Caribbean Tourism Research Centre

General perspective

This paper attempts to analyse the growth prospects for the tourist sector in the Commonwealth Caribbean in the next five years with specific reference to the implications for employment, flows of earnings, investment, and economic development as a whole. The Commonwealth Caribbean countries considered are St Kitts-Nevis-Anguilla, Antigua, St Lucia, Dominica, St Vincent, Grenada, Montserrat (normally referred to as the LDCs) and Jamaica, Barbados, and Trinidad and Tobago (the MDCs).

International tourism has assumed major proportions in the past decade. High incomes in developed countries, increasing leisure time, and until recently a lowering of air fares, owing to the introduction of the more efficient jet aircraft, have in different ways contributed to the high rate of growth of tourist traffic. From 1950 until the present, international tourist expenditures grew at an estimated average rate of 12% a year. International tourist receipts (excluding international fare payments) were $2.1 billion in 1950. In 1973 they had reached $27.6 billion.[1] Over the same period international tourist arrivals grew from 25 million to 215 million, an average annual growth of 11%. It has been argued that the average annual growth rate of tourist expenditure for the period 1950-1966 was more than double that of national incomes of industrialised countries.[2] The average annual rate of growth of tourism exceeded the average growth rate of world trade (1950-1973) by 3.5% and per capita income growth by 3% annually for the same period.[3]

This spectacular growth has been dominated by the industrialised countries, which are the main tourist-receiving and tourist-generating areas. These fifteen countries account for 70% of the world demand for tourism. The developing countries' share of international tourist arrivals was as low as 13.8% in 1973 and their share of international tourist receipts 13.3%. Although the former represented an increase

1 International Union of Tourist Organisations (IUOTO)—Statistics.
2 John M. Bryden, *Tourism and Development: A Case Study of the Commonwealth Caribbean*, London, Cambridge University Press, 1973.
3 IUOTO.

Table 1. Distribution of passenger flow to selected CARICOM countries, 1969-74

	1969	1970	1971	1972	1973	1974	Total
Antigua	61,261	65,369	67,637	72,328	72,786	69,854	409,235
Dominica	8,246	12,450	14,429	16,803	17,558	18,996	88,482
Grenada	26,627	30,436	35,626	37,933	33,490	14,723	181,835
Montserrat	7,475	8,382	7,270	11,463	10,727	10,754	56,071
St Kitts-Nevis-Anguilla	11,779	13,472	15,105	16,245	14,937	13,251	84,789
St Lucia	25,482	29,529	33,198	42,399	45,399	51,816	227,823
St Vincent	12,690	15,820	15,368	15,701	15,594	19,242	94,415
LDC total	156,560	175,458	188,633	212,872	210,491	198,636	1,142,650
Growth rate (%)	12	12	8	13	—1	—6	5
Jamaica	276,929	309,122	359,323	407,806	418,257	432,987	2,204,424
Trinidad and Tobago	95,620	86,890	111,340	114,550	125,640	129,000	663,040
Barbados	134,303	156,417	189,075	210,349	222,080	230,718	1,142,942
MDC total	506,852	552,429	659,738	732,705	765,977	792,705	4,010,406
Growth rate (%)	...	9	19	11	5	3	9
Total	663,412	727,887	848,371	945,577	976,468	991,341	5,153,056
of which: LDC (%)	24	24	22	23	22	20	22
MDC (%)	75	76	78	78	79	80	78

from 7.3% in 1962, the latter was down on that year's 18.8% share — ie average expenditure per visitor had fallen (according to IUOTO studies from $245.8 in 1962 to $121.3 in 1973).

Tourism has become an attractive investment for many Caribbean countries. It has the potential to provide much-needed foreign exchange and employment opportunities, to broaden the developmental base through a dispersion of industrial activity, and to stimulate economic development in general.

At the tenth Commonwealth Caribbean Summit, held in St Kitts in December 1975, the area's current account deficit (excluding Trinidad and Tobago) was projected at EC$1,000m in 1976, the non-oil countries of the MDC group (Jamaica, Barbados, and Guyana) accounting for EC$750m and the less developed countries EC$250m. Trinidad and Tobago alone would earn a surplus — of EC$2.5 billion. The present situation, and the short- and medium-term prospects, of a major foreign exchange earner — the major one in a number of islands — is all the more significant.

Pattern and distribution of tourist flow to the Commonwealth Caribbean — future prospects

Over the period 1969-74 the CARICOM countries of the Commonwealth Caribbean generated a total volume of 5,153,056 tourists. Table 1 shows the distribution of arrivals among the Commonwealth Caribbean countries covered during this period and the growth rates of the two groups, the MDCs and the LDCs. Table 2 shows the growth rates in the individual countries and their share of total arrivals.

A particularly significant feature is that in 1973 no country in the group recorded more than 10% growth (the highest rate was that of Trinidad, which has a high concentration of business and inter-Caribbean traffic). 1974 saw some recovery, but only two, minor destinations recorded above 10% expansion. The figures used so far relate to number of arrivals only. It is tourist days, rather than arrivals, which must be considered. One example illustrates the sometimes signficant divergence betwen the two. In 1973 Grenada recorded an inflow of 37,933 tourists and St Lucia 42,399. It would seem that St Lucia enjoyed a better tourist season than Grenada. But if average length of stay is taken into account — twelve days for Grenada and less than four days for St Lucia — there were 455,196 tourist days in Grenada, more than double the 169,596 tourist days in St Lucia.

The pattern of distribution of traffic throughout the countries has remained relatively constant for the period 1969-74, with Jamaica, Barbados, Trinidad and Tobago, and Antigua, in that order, consistently dominating the traffic volume. The historic inability of any country

Table 2. The rate of growth in tourism for selected CARICOM countries and share of tourist arrivals, 1969-74

	1970	1971	1972	1973	1974	Average 1969-74	Share of total
Antigua	6.7	3.4	6.9	0.6	— 3.7	2.9	8.0
Dominica	5.1	15.9	16.5	4.4	8.1	19.2	1.7
Grenada	2.7	17.1	6.5	—11.7	—56.0	— 8.3	3.5
St Kitts-Nevis-Anguilla	14.4	12.1	7.5	— 8.1	—11.3	2.9	1.6
Montserrat	12.1	—13.3	57.6	— 6.4	— 3.0	9.0	1.0
St Lucia	15.9	12.4	27.5	8.2	13.1	15.4	4.4
St Vincent	24.7	— 2.8	2.2	— 0.7	23.4	9.4	1.8
Barbados	16.5	20.9	11.3	5.6	3.9	11.6	22.2
Jamaica	11.6	16.2	13.5	2.6	3.5	9.5	42.8
Trinidad and Tobago	— 9.1	28.1	2.8	9.7	2.7	6.8	13.0

Table 3 shows country-ranking under the two measures.

Table 3. Ranking by number of tourists and by tourist days 1974

	Ranking by number of tourists	Ranking by tourist days
Antigua	4	5
Barbados	2	2
Dominica	7	10
Grenada	8	4*
Jamaica	1	1
Montserrat	10	8
St Kitts-Nevis-Anguilla	9	9
St Lucia	5	6
St Vincent	6	7
Trinidad and Tobago	3	3

*1973

significantly to alter the distribution of tourist flows to the region has very important implications for policy revision.

Air transport and marketing policy and planning

One of the basic constraints to tourism growth in most of the LDCs is the inadequacy of the air transportation system. Over 95% of tourists to the region travel by air. It is no coincidence that Jamaica, Barbados, and Trinidad and Tobago, the countries that dominate traffic to the region, are the only countries in the group that own national airlines. While it would not be economical for each country to have its own airline, flights between the group need to be rescheduled and frequencies improved.[1]

The high percentage of inter-Caribbean travellers on Leewards Islands Air Transport, the regional carrier which theoretically provides 96 seats per day (two flights of a 48-seat Avro), reduces the ability of the air transport system to cater for tourists from other destinations, even if different connections are provided by other international gateways. (In addition to the three MDCs mentioned, St Lucia, Antigua and St Kitts-Nevis are served by international flights). The problem is complicated by the fact that the routing schedule is not consistent with the traffic flow patterns betwen the combinations of cities served by the airlines. The inability of scheduled air traffic to service the number of tourists necessary for a viable tourism industry in the islands of the Eastern Caribbean has made these islands very dependent on charter flights. The emergence of the one-stop tour charter (OTC) is of particular significance, since it reduces the host country's control over the market image of its tourism product. Yet the viability of the industry in each individual country depends upon maintaining control over promotion so that it can sufficiently differentiate itself from other destinations in ways meaningful to the consumer and to the destination itself. The tour operators' interests may not fit in with national or regional long-range policy.

However, the one-stop tour charter provides a package which satisfies the buyer, in that it reduces the uncertainty that is always associated with travel to an unknown destination, it is economical, and it is convenient. Any strategy to preempt the tour operator must involve meeting all these requirements. This in particular weights the situation against the small islands in the Caribbean. It is a question of cost and expertise and the ability to run effectively foreign-based travel agencies.

Marketing policy

Marketing is one of the traditional weaknesses of Caribbean tourism. However, as international tourism becomes more competitive, the more

---

1 See Caribbean Tourism Research Centre, *Caribbean Air Transportation System*, published in 1975, for an exhaustive treatment of this problem.

will the future of the Caribbean industry depend on effective marketing. In this respect there is an urgent need for each country to identify its national tourism product, and then follow this up with an appropriate marketing and promotion policy. Since consumer priorities change with time, this policy must also be flexible.

While the effectiveness of tourism policy is not linearly related to money spent (in most instances a basic amount of outlay is required, below which returns are minimal), the historic distribution patterns of tourism in the Caribbean show a rough approximation to financial commitments by countries. The cold facts are that the fall in the LDC share of the CARICOM market must be arrested, even at a time when their budgetary position has worsened.

The major market segments

The Caribbean has traditionally been an attractive destination for US travellers — ranking second only to Europe and the Mediterranean. In 1960. 39.2% of US citizens who travelled overseas went to the West Indies and Central America, while 50.9% went to Europe and the Mediterranean. In 1970 the figures were respectively 31.6% and 55.1%.[1] Table 4 shows the US share of the Caribbean tourist market. It is notable that since 1969 this share has shown (in general) a gradual decline for all the countries considered, except St. Lucia, St. Vincent, and Jamaica, where it has been relatively constant. For all other countries the US share has declined by around 10 percentage points. Over the period the average annual growth rate of this market sector has been only 3.2%.

The main offsetting factor has been the growth of inter-Caribbean travel (10.5%) and to a much smaller extent the growth of the Canadian market sector (19%). The volume of tourism from Canada is still very low compared to that from the USA (see Table 6). The inter-Caribbean segment has shown the most significant growth (see Table 7). It is the leading segment or a very high contributor to tourism growth in all the LDCs. In Trinidad for special reasons (business and commercial traffic) it has the largest share. The UK and European contribution to the growth of Caribbean tourism borders on the negligable, except in St Lucia where the UK tourist has the dominant share of the market.

Owing to the fluctuating patterns in the growth rates of the various important market segments, it is difficult to predict future performance. Assuming recovery from the last two years' trend and a restoration of growth in the US market, expansion in the range of 5% to 10% could be achieved annually.

---

1 US Department of Commerce, based on data of US Department of Justice, Immigration and Naturalization Service.

Table 4. US share of the CARICOM tourist market, 1969-74

	1969	1970	1971	1972	1973	1974
			% of total arrivals			
Antigua	52.7	48.0	45.2	44.9	43.2	43.1
Dominica	27.1	22.9	24.09	16.2	26.7	20.7
Grenada	36.6	36.8	34.9	34.7	34.8	27.5
Montserrat	41.5	35.5	35.5	33.5	38.9	23.6
St Lucia	22	26.4	23.1	18.3	24.5	23.2
St Kitts-Nevis	33.8	28.9	26.6	25.5	27.2	25.6
St Vincent	36.7	36.4	36.3	36.8	40.3	38.8
Barbados	39.2	36.5	36.2	35.9	33	28.2
Jamaica	77.3	77.5	87.4	77.5	77.8	78
Trinidad and Tobago	34.5	35.7	32.3	27.6	25.8	25
			numbers			
Antigua	32,276	31,786	30,553	32,456	31,467	30,353
Dominica	2,238	2,850	3,476	2,719	4,696	3,928
Grenada	10,862	11,214	12,441	13,157	11,665	4,044
Montserrat	3,303	3,417	3,219	4,199	4,915	3,036
St Lucia	5,614	7,807	7,666	7,756	11,359	12,039
St Kitts-Nevis	3,988	3,890	4,023	4,151	4,038	3,390
St Vincent	4,664	5,765	5,581	5,786	6,288	7,471
Barbados	52,689	57,111	68,487	75,525	73,280	66,237
Jamaica	214,140	245,689	292,460	316,191	325,315	339,694
Trinidad and Tobago	33,060	31,020	36,050	30,770	32,450	32,300

Table 5. Annual growth rate of the US segment of the Caribbean tourist market, 1970-74

(percentages)

	1970	1971	1972	1973	1974	Average
Antigua	— 1.7	— 3.6	6.2	— 3.0	— 4.2	— 1.3
Barbados	8.3	0.2	10.3	— 3.0	— 9.6	1.6
Dominica	2.7	0.2	10.3	3.0	— 9.6	1.6
Grenada	3.2	10.7	5.7	—11.3	—65.0	— 9.3
Jamaica	14.7	19.0	8.1	2.8	4.4	9.8
Montserrat	3.4	— 5.8	30.4	17.0	—38.2	1.4
St Kitts-Nevis	2.4	3.4	3.2	2.2	—16.5	— 1.1
St Lucia	39.0	— 1.8	1.2	46.4	5.9	17.9
St Vincent	23.6	3.2	3.7	1.6	18.8	10.2
Trinidad and Tobago	— 6.2	16.2	—14.6	5.4	— 0.4	0.1

Table 6. Canadian arrivals in the CARICOM tourist market, 1969-74

	1969	1970	1971	1972	1973	1974
			Numbers			
Antigua	7,537	7,107	6,958	8,397	10,070	9,781
Dominica	431	1,046	808	776	826	943
Grenada	3,419	3,759	4,662	5,431	4,134	1,535
St Kitts-Nevis	753	893	790	1,022	820	997
Montserrat	710	1,116	917	1,279	1,513	929
St Lucia	2,547	2,928	3,376	4,406	8,785	9,844
St Vincent	1,270	1,436	1,245	1,122	1,333	1,574
Barbados	31,617	39,609	53,690	61,918	68,712	77,246
Jamaica	27,101	25,164	28,165	38,331	36,867	37,445
Trinidad and Tobago	9,440	7,270	11,030	8.590	10,980	11,470
			Percentage annual change			
Antigua		5.6	— 2.1	20.7	19.9	— 2.9
Dominica		142.7	22.5	— 4	— 6	14
Grenada		9.9	4.6	16.5	—23.9	—62.9
St Kitts-Nevis		18.6	—11.5	29.4	18.3	—38.5
Montserrat		57.2	—17.8	39.4	18.3	—38.6
St Lucia		14.9	15.3	30.5	99.4	12.5
St Vincent		13.3	—13.3	9.1	—18.8	18.1
Barbados		25.3	35.5	16.0	11.0	12.4
Jamaica		— 0.1	11.9	36.1	—38.0	1.6
Trinidad and Tobago		—23.0	51.7	—22.0	—26.6	4.4

Table 7. Annual growth rate of inter-Caribbean segment of CARICOM tourist market, 1970-74 (%)

	1970	1971	1972	1973	1974	Average
Antigua	27.6	30.8	— 1.0	— 2.0	— 5.3	10.0
Barbados	29.0	2.6	7.3	7.8	— 4.1	8.5
Dominica	51.0	25.7	43.6	—19	— 3.0	19.7
Grenada	— 6.0	21.5	3.6	— 6.7	—53.9	— 8.3
Jamaica	9.9	12.0	57.7	10.0	— 6.7	16.6
Montserrat	40.1	— 9.8	37.7	—12.6	50.9	19.3
St Kitts-Nevis-Anguilla	23.0	18.7	7.6	—11.2	—13.4	4.9
St Lucia	23.2	18.7	36.9	—32.6	—10.0	7.2
St Vincent	23.5	17,2	4.4	—14.0	15.2	9.3
Trinidad and Tobago	— 5.7	24.3	—43.8	18.8	5.6	17.4

Recommendations

(1) Immediate consideration should be given to the cost and benefit of the development of a regional airline system, and to the terms of sharing financial commitments and expertise.

(2) In view of budget constraints in the LDCs, the feasibility of multi-centre holiday marketing should be assessed.

(3) There is immediate need for proper data collection. Timing, consistency, methodology, accuracy and form of presentation need to be improved, and the scope and structure of data collection altered.

Demand and supply of accommodation in the Commonwealth Caribbean: projections on future profitability and planning policy

The analysis that follows is intended to serve a dual purpose: an essessment of the relationship between the supply and demand for accommodation, and the formulation of an approach to planning hotel construction in the future.

The argument put forward in the next few pages rests on the concept of the operative or functional maximum supply of accommodation. Briefly, this distinguishes between the theoretical maximum supply of accommodation as determined by the number of bed-nights (beds x 365) and the operative maximum. Assuming that there are only 10 hotel beds in a country, theoretically in any one year its hotel plant can accommodate 3,650 persons. This assumes 100% occupancy and that each person stays one night. However, in itself, this is not a very valuable figure for planning hotel building. The important variable to be introduced is the average length of stay. If the average length of stay is ten days, the operative maximum is 3,650 ÷ 10 or 365. If the average length of stay increases, the maximum will decrease, ie the operative maximum will vary inversely with the average length of stay. In actual fact a monthly disaggregated data analysis provides better information and is necessary, especially with the monthly fluctuations in tourist arrivals. This could be calculated by multiplying the number of beds available by the days in the month and then dividing by the average length of stay for that particular month. The resulting operative maximum supply of accommodation must then be compared with the respective monthly demand for accommodation; thus in this case, $\frac{10 \times 30}{10} = 30$. The operative maximum is thus 30 for the month in question. Since the average length of stay will vary, the constraints on the number of persons that can be accommodated will also change. Table 8 illustrates the variables involved in this process. The figure for maximum capacity is arrived at by multiplying the total number of beds by 365 and dividing by the average length of stay.

The figure for excess or under-capacity is derived by subtracting demand (ie actual arrivals x average length of stay) from maximum annual capacity. The annual occupancy rate is calculated by dividing demand for accommodation by maximum annual capacity.

Table 8. Estimates of utilisation of hotel capacity, 1974

	No. of beds	Average length of stay	Maximum annual capacity	Demand for accom-moda-tion	Estimated annual excess* or under capacity	Estimated hotel occu-pancy
Antigua	2,644	4	241,265	69,854	—171,411	28.9
Barbados	8.453	6	514,224	230,718	—283,506	44.9
Dominica	341	4	31,116	18,996	— 12,120	61.0
Grenada	1,800	12	54,750	33,490[1]	— 21,260[2]	61.0[3]
Jamaica	21,951	8	1,001,514	432,987	—568,527	43.2
Montserrat	226	8	10,311	10,754	+ 443	Constraint
St Kitts-Nevis	930	9	37,716	13,251	— 24,465	35.1
St Lucia	2,948	3.5	307,434	58,816	—248,615	19.0
St Vincent	842	8	38,416	79,242	— 19,174	50.0
Trinidad and Tobago	3,140	5.5	208,381	129,000	— 79,381	61.9

* Indicates under-capacity; + indicates fully utilised capacity.
1 In 1973.
2 Under-capacity is 41,740 using 1974 statistics.
3 Occupancy is equal to 26.9% using 1974 statistics.
Sources: Tourist Boards; Shankland Cox, *Supply of Tourism in the Caribbean*, Study for the World Bank, 1973.

These estimates indicate a high percentage of under-utilised hotel capacity in the Commonwealth Caribbean. In this respect St Lucia, Antigua and St Kitts-Nevis emerge as the most critically offending cases. It is estimated that for an A-class hotel break-even is in the range of 60%. (If this is in fact true only three countries achieve this average.) In fact the break-even could be at a much higher level, since this estimate of break-even assumed winter prices. Hotels in the Caribbean are very clearly going through a stage of extreme financial hardship, the exact extent depending in individual national cases on the distribution of hotel type, the capital inputs involved, and the rate of utilisation of capacity. Column five indicates the demand that needs to be generated to fill the excess capacity at 1974 average length of stay.

For both the MDCs and the LDCs as a group, the average occupancy level is estimated to be 50%. However, since the share of the tourist market in the LDCs by Caribbean travellers is greater, the actual demand for accommodation could be smaller than arrivals figures suggest.

Over the last five years the Caribbean segment of the tourist market in LDCs and Trinidad has emerged in most cases as the main contributor to the growth in the volume of traffic. This has important implications (beside the fact that such traffic flows amount to a redistribution of revenue in the area and not a net addition) for seasonal patterns of travel, expenditure, and average length-of-stay patterns. Caribbean visitors demand accommodation mainly in the summer when lower prices prevail, and when consequently the break-even occupancy will be higher.

Table 9. Inter-Caribbean share of the CARICOM tourist market

	(%)
Antigua	28
Barbados	16
Dominica	53
Grenada	33
Jamaica	3
Montserrat	50
St Kitts-Nevis	57
St Lucia	21
St Vincent	38
Trinidad and Tobago	39

Assuming that roughly 50% of Caribbean travellers require accommodation, demand for accommodation is estimated as shown in Table 10. The occupancy rate shown is consequently lower, and more realistic.

Table 10. Estimates of effective demand for accommodation, 1974

	Deduction 1974 tourist figure	Estimated percentage demanding accommo-tion	Estimated actual demand	Estimated maximum annual capacity	Estimated occupancy rate (%)
Antigua	69,854	93	64,964	241,265	27.9
Barbados	250,718	95	219,182	514,224	42.6
Dominica	18,996	72	13,964	31,116	44.9
Grenada	33,490[1]	85	28,466	54,750	52.0
Jamaica	423,987	100	432,987	1,001,514	43.2(22.8[2])
Montserrat	10,754	75	8,065	10,311	78.0
St Kitts-Nevis	13,251	70	9,275	37,716	24.6
St Lucia	51,516	90	46,634	307,434	15.2
St Vincent	19,242	80	15,393	38,416	40.1
Trinidad and Tobago	129,000	80	103,200	208,381	49.5

1 1973.
2 Occupancy level based upon 1974 data.

Fixed unit costs fall as occupancy increases. These costs vary with size of establishment. The contribution margin per room varies according to a number of factors, eg employee-room productivity and other efficiency factors and the price per room (or revenue per bed-night). Consequently different occupancy levels will have varying impacts on different-size establishments. Consequently the overall utilisation rate is a figure which does not indicate the impact on profitability in specific cases.

Assuming:	Fixed cost	$100,000.00
	Revenue per bed-night	100.00
	Contribution margin per bed-night	10%
	No. of occupants required to break even	$\frac{FC}{CM} = \frac{100,000}{10}$

$$= 10,000$$

If the annual capacity of the hotel is equal to 20,000 bed-nights, then break-even in this case is 50%.

If price decreases, as it does in summer, revenue per bed-night and the contribution margin fall. Occupancy levels will have to increase if break-even is to be achieved. For example, if the contribution margin falls to 5%, 20,000 bed-nights will be needed — ie 100% utilisation. The problem consequently becomes critical if low prices persist for too long.

The estimates in Tables 8 and 9 indicate that to fill the excess capacity the region has immediately to generate in the range of 1,408,192 to 1,502,997 additional tourists with the existing average length-of-stay pattern for each country, although not in the same historical distribution pattern[1] of arrivals that the region has experienced over the last five years. For example, Antigua and St Lucia, which in 1969-74 received 8% and 4.4% respectively of tourists coming to the Caribbean, need to secure 11.7% and 17.3% respectively of the additional number of tourists to be generated in the Caribbean to utilise fully even their existing hotel capacity. Regionally there are thus two interrelated objectives: (1) to generate the required traffic, (2) to allocate the traffic generated in the required proportion to fill excess capacity. Table 11 shows the share of additional demand which would need to be allocated to the various countries (under both demand assumptions in Table 9 and 10) to fill existing capacity. The figures in the final column are particularly significant when compared to actual growth rates in recent years (see Table 2), which are clearly too low to fill existing capacity in the next five years.

1 See Table 1.

Table 11. Estimate of required growth rates, 1976-79

	Table 9 Estimate of excess capacity	Table 10 Modified estimate of excess capacity	Percentage of total excess capacity		Historic distribution pattern	Annual growth rate required to fill existing capacity in five years
	(A)	(B)	(A)	(B)		
Antigua	171,411	176,301	12.2	11.7	8.0	30
Dominica	12,120	17,152	0.01	1.1	1.7	17
Grenada	21,260	26,152	1.5	1.1	3.5	13
Montserrat	0	2,246	0	0.15	1.0	1
St Kitts-Nevis	24,464	28,441	1.7	1.9	1.6	32
St Vincent	19,174	23,023	1.4	1.5	1.8	20
St Lucia	248,618	260,800	17.6	17.3	4.4	45
LDC total	497,048	534,247				
Barbados	283,506	295,042	20.1	19.6	22.2	18
Jamaica	568,257	568,527	40.5	37.8	42.8	18
Trinidad and Tobago	79,381	105,381	5.6	7.0	13.0	15
MDC total	831,144	968,750				
LDC + MDC total	1,408,192	1,502,997				

In fact at present growth rates the addition of 2,445,121 tourists (an increase of 146%) will not be achieved even in the next ten years.

Profitability picture

The actual gross revenue attained in hotels for the various countries is estimated in Table 12 by multiplying the number of persons demanding accommodation (the 1974 tourist figure is used after applying the correction factor for inter-Caribbean travellers) by the average length of stay, and then by the estimated revenue per bed-night ($40).

Table 12. Estimates of gross hotel revenue, 1974

	Estimated demand	Average length of stay	Estimated actual gross revenue $
Antigua	64,964	4	10,394,240
Barbados	219,182	8	70,138,240
Dominica	13,964	5	2,792,800
Grenada	28,466*	13	14,346,864
Jamaica	432,987	9	155,875,320
Montserrat	8,065	10	3,226,000
St Kitts-Nevis	9,275	9	3,339,000
St Lucia	46,634	5	9,326,800
St Vincent	15,393	8	4,925,760
Trinidad and Tobago	103,200	6	24,760,000

* 1973.

Table 13 estimates the maximum gross revenue attainable by multiplying the total number of bed-nights available by the estimated revenue per bed-night.

Table 13. Estimate of maximum attainable gross hotel revenue, 1974

	Bed-nights	Maximum obtainable gross revenue $
Antigua	965,060	38,602,400
Barbados	3,085,345	123,413,800
Dominica	124,456	4,978,600
Grenada	657,000	26,280,000
Jamaica	8,012,115	320,484,600
Montserrat	82,490	3,299,600
St Kitts-Nevis	339,450	13,578,000
St Lucia	1,076,020	43,040,500
St Vincent	307,330	12,293,200
Trinidad and Tobago	1,146,100	45,844,000

Table 14 estimates the amount of gross revenue foregone owing to under-utilisation of capacity. In total the CARICOM countries have an ungenerated gross revenue-earning capacity of approximately $332,669,904. Net profits as a percentage of gross revenue differ from hotel to hotel and country to country (because of different fixed capital inputs and efficiency ratios) but in general range from 8% to 12%. However, net profits could accumulate only after the break-even point has been achieved. As shown before, not many hotels achieve a break-even point of 60%.

Table 14. Estimate of gross revenue foregone, 1974

	Estimated maximum attainable gross hotel revenue $	Estimated actual gross hotel revenue $	Difference $	Percentage of gross revenue unattained
	$	$	$	
Antigua	38,602,400	10,394,240	28,208,160	73.1
Barbados	123,413,800	70,138,240	53,255,460	43.2
Dominica	4,978,600	2,792,800	2,185,800	43.9
Grenada	26,280,000	14,346,864	11,933,136	45.9
Jamaica	320,484,600	155,875,320	154,609,280	51.4
Montserrat	3,299,600	3,226,000	73,699	2.2
St Kitts-Nevis	13,578,000	3,339,000	10,239,000	78.3
St Lucia	43,040,800	9,326,800	33,714,000	78.3
St Vincent	12,293,200	4,925,762	7,367,440	59.9
Trinidad and Tobago	45,844,000	24,760,000	21,084,000	46.0

It is recognised that building, wages, and materials costs differ from island to island. It must also be admitted that the estimates of room cost found in a number of sources range from $12,000 to $30,000 per room. However, owing to lack of data and to facilitate further analysis, it is assumed in Table 15 that the cost per room is $30,000 (including land and fixtures).

Table 15. Estimate of hotels' maximum net profit, 1974

	No. of rooms	Total value of investment (1 x $30,000)	Maximum attainable gross revenue (Table 13)	Maximum net profit at 10%
Antigua	1,322	39,600,000	38,602,400	3,860,240
Barbados	4,226	126,780,000	123,413,800	12,341,380
Dominica	170	5,100,000	4,978,600	497,860
Grenada	900	27,000,000	26,280,000	2,628,800
Jamaica	10,975	329,250,000	320,484,600	32,048,460
Montserrat	113	44,220,000	43,040,800	4,304,800
St Kitts-Nevis	465	13,950,000	13,578,000	1,357,800
St Lucia	1,474	44,220,000	43,040,800	4,304,800
St Vincent	421	12,630,000	13,293,200	1,229,320
Trinidad and Tobago	1,570	47,100,000	45,844,000	4,584,400

Future prospects — hotel construction planning and policy

Let us assume a 5% and 10% annual growth rate for the various

Commonwealth Caribbean countries and examine its implications for profitability and planning policy in the hotel industry and tourism as a whole.

Table 16. Projections of tourist arrivals, 1975-80

		1975	1976	1977	1978	1979	1980
Antigua	5%	73,347	77,014	80,684	84,908	89,153	93,611
	10%	78,800	83,435	81,778	100,955	111,094	122,203
Barbados	5%	242,254	254,366	267,084	280,449	294,461	309,184
	10%	253,789	279,168	307,085	337,294	371,574	408,730
Dominica	5%	19,945	20,943	22,011	23,112	24,267	25,480
	10%	20,895	22,985	25,284	27,812	30,593	33,652
Grenada	5%	35,164	36,922	38,786	40,707	42,743	44,879
	10%	36,840	40,523	44,575	49,033	53,936	59,323
Jamaica	5%	454,636	477,368	501,236	526,298	552,613	580,244
	10%	476,285	523,914	576,305	633,936	697,330	767,062
Montserrat	5%	11,290	11,855	12,450	13,068	13,720	14,406
	10%	11,829	13,012	14,313	15,745	17,319	19,051
St Kitts-Nevis	5%	13,913	14,609	15,396	16,106	16,912	17,257
	10%	14,576	16,037	17,637	19,400	21,340	23,474
St Lucia	5%	54,407	57,127	59,983	62,982	66,132	69,438
	10%	56,997	62,697	68,987	75,863	83,450	91,795
St Vincent	5%	20,204	21,214	22,275	23,388	24,558	25,786
	10%	21,166	23,283	25,611	28,172	30,989	34,085
Trinidad and	5%	135,450	142,222	149,336	156,800	164,640	172,872
and Tobago	10%	141,900	156,090	171,700	188,869	207,756	228,531

Assuming that depreciation is insignificant and that hotel construction remains constant,[1] the occupancy levels shown in Table 17 are projected to be maintained until 1980 (without adjustment for the inter-Caribbean share).

On these projections Montserrat is the only country for which hotel building is an immediate urgency. For the year 1975 it has already surpassed its maximum attainable supply and is likely to run into constraints in accommodation facilities. Although Dominica, Grenada, and Trinidad and Tobago could achieve 80% by 1980, the rate of increase is in fact so slow that there is likely to be some leeway before the accommodation supply becomes a constraint. If 10% annual growth is realised, Montserrat, Dominica, Trinidad and Tobago, Grenada, and to a lesser extent St Vincent will become candidates for hotel building projects.

Critical areas like St. Lucia, Antigua, Jamaica, St Kitts, and Barbados should place hotel building under stringent control unless they can

1 Jamaica is in the process of building 1,112 rooms to be in operation in 1976. During the writing of this report a moratorum on hotel building was set in Jamaica, except in the Negril area.

Table 17. Projections of hotel occupancy rates, 1975-80

	1975	1976	1977	1978	1979	1980	1975	1976	1977	1978	1979	1980
	5% annual growth						10% annual growth					
Antigua	30.4	31.9	33.5	35.2	36.9	38.8	32.7	34.6	38.0	41.8	46.0	51.0
Barbados	47.1	49.4	51.9	54.3	57.3	60.1	49.3	54.2	59.7	65.7	72.8	78.0
Dominica	64.0	67.3	70.7	74.2	77.9	81.8	67.1	73.8	81.2	89.3	98.3	108.0
Grenada	64.2	67.4	70.8	74.4	78.1	82.0	67.3	74.0	81.4	89.6	98.5	109.0
Jamaica	45.4	47.6	50.0	52.5	55.2	57.9	47.5	52.3	57.6	63.3	69.6	76.0
Montserrat	109.4	114.9	120.7	126.7	133.0	139.7	114.7	126.1	133.8	152.7	167.9	185.0
St Kitts-Nevis	36.8	38.7	40.8	42.7	44.8	45.7	38.6	42.5	46.7	51.4	56.6	62.0
St Lucia	17.7	18.6	19.5	20.5	21.5	22.6	18.5	20.4	22.4	24.7	27.1	30.0
St Vincent	52.5	55.2	57.9	60.8	63.9	67.1	55.0	60.6	66.6	73.3	80.6	89.0
Trinidad and Tobago	65.0	68.3	71.7	75.3	79.0	83.0	68.0	74.9	82.4	90.6	99.7	110.0

increase the average length of stay significantly or achieve a higher annual growth than 10% before 1980.

At the national level the actual decision to build could, of course, involve considerations of ownership, prospective costs and revenues, the rate at which full capacity is presently being approached, national policies and the general future prospects of tourism.

The average arrival occupancy figure represents the mean of a distribution with extreme end values of the foreign-owned chain hotel, commanding a decent occupancy level year-round, and the small indigenous hotel obtaining very low occupancy levels. This is substantiated by the data for hotels in the top twenty occupancy range in Jamaica — six in Kingston, ten in Montego Bay, and four in Ocho Rios.[1] These hotels average approximately 27 percentage points above the national average.

There is a Caribbean-wide concern for the plight of the small hoteliers who have found themselves in difficulty owing to the structure of their debt obligations, interest charges, and decreasing earnings or increasing losses. There is presently under review the question of rescheduling the financial obligations of the small hoteliers by replacing either short- or medium-term debt by longer-run or more flexible financial obligations. This is another case of the lack of financial institutions in the Commonwealth Caribbean to provide long-term financing for critical industries. It has also been suggested that their equity be increased. However, changes in capital structure do not alter the earning capacity of the small hoteliers, and this is the test of long-run viability.

In an attempt to solve the problem of the small indigenous hoteliers, the concept of a holiday village is now being pursued. This involves a rationalisation of administrative, financial and sporting facilities for ten hotels of twenty rooms each. Although this concept has intuitive appeal, sufficient research has not been done to determine its feasibility.

There are critical questions that need to be answered. How do the cost and revenue functions for various-size hotels compare? What is the optimum administrative size for various sizes of hotel or hotels of various categories? At what rate do these hotels approach break-even, and what is the rate of profit accumulation after the break-even? There is also a need to analyse the occupancy distribution for various types of hotel and the reason for such levels of occupancy.

The future of the hotel industry in the Caribbean is difficult to predict. There is need for firm national policies on hotel building. The concept of holiday villages has appeal but much more research must be done to determine the range of average cost within which such hotels will be operating and the real benefits associated with the concept. There is also

---

1 Data on ownership of these hotels were not available at the time of writing. A good guess is that foreign ownership predominates.

need to raise the net social benefit by reducing the degree of foreign ownership and to increase the return on the capital employed.

Recommendations

(1) Efforts must be made immediately at the national level to control hotel building in Jamaica, Barbados, Antigua, St Lucia, and St Kitts-Nevis.

(2) Future national policy on hotel building should be firmly laid down. Particular emphasis should be placed on the need to revise hotel incentives acts so that they favour only nationals.

(3) Research should be carried out immediately to determine the behaviour of cost and revenue functions in various types of hotel.

(4) Marketing of tourism must integrate facility development, under local ownership, with the socio-economic characteristics of visitors.

(5) The refinancing of small hotels needs careful supervision. Viability must be understood to be dependent on operating features and capacity, not on financial structure.

General economic prospects of the tourism sector

All the Commonwealth Caribbean countries are small and consequently face a physical constraint on economic growth and development — through the limitation on resources of land and population. Economic activities have been competitive instead of complementary with each other. This is demonstrated in Antigua where tourism has grown at the expense of the agriculture sector. The LDCs all possess a similar economic structure. Except for Trinidad and Tobago (oil, natural gas, pitch), Jamaica (bauxite), and to some extent Barbados (natural gas), mineral deposits are lacking in commercially exploitable quantities. The other countries are left with the problem of generating employment and income from the production of bananas and sugar (to some extent in addition cocoa, coffee, copra, arrowroot, nutmeg, cotton, and ginger) at a sufficiently high level to maintain a minimum acceptable standard of living and to earn enough foreign currency to increase productive capacity through locally-financed capital investments. The imbalance and lack of complementarity in the resource endowments of the islands of the Commonwealth Caribbean, especially the LDCs, have made these countries very highly foreign-trade oriented and at the same time narrowed the scope for effective import substitution policies. The relatively stagnant and (to some extent) declining agricultural sector has not taken advantage of the increases in world prices of sugar and bananas since 1973. Higher prices have not evoked significant increases in supply. The higher contribution of the agricultural sector, where attained, has thus been mainly a result of increased price rather than volume. In short the LDCs have not generated sufficient foreign capital, or provided a significant level of employment and income even with their present dependence on foreign aid, foreign private capital, and grants. Recurrent budget expenditure has also exceeded recurrent revenue since 1971 for the group as a whole, and for each country separately since 1973. It is in this context that tourism is regarded as the only alternative means of development where it may be used (as a short- to medium-term strategy to generate foreign exchange to finance capital projects, create employment, and induce growth in other sectors).

Tourism components can be divided into five main categories:[1]

(1) natural resources;

(2) infrastructure;

(3) transportation and transportation equipment;

(4) superstructure;

(5) hospitality resources.

Tourism thus consists of an interdependent system of activities. Benefits and costs occur through the input created by the interaction of tourism and the household, production, and government sectors of the economy. Such interaction affects the level and distribution of income, government revenue, the balance of payments, and the diversification of economic activity. Consequently a useful approach for analysing the costs and benefits of the growth of tourism is the concept of economic linkage, which envisages tourism interacting with the economy through the primary trades, and the supportive activities supplying the primary trades, and with the rest of the economy, through economic flows and transactions.

Table 18 shows the inter-industry matrix for Barbados (in 1968). The weak linkage of tourism with the rest of the economy is spotlighted by the fact that the contribution of agriculture to tourism is only 5.2% and of construction 1.5%. This weak inter-industry linkage is characteristic of the open economics of the Commonwealth Caribbean, and the indications are that such linkages are still weaker in the LDCs.

The strongest link established has been with the rest of the world. This fact is substantiated by estimates of the import co-efficient of a dollar of tourist expenditure to be 42 cents[2], 34 cents[3], and 50 cents of the tourist dollar in Barbados, Jamaica, and St Vincent respectively. In the other islands of the LDCs it is certainly in the range of 50 cents. Even though tourism by its nature has the potential to provide balanced growth, the experience of the economies in the Caribbean is that growth, if any, has been anything but balanced.

---

1 Robert W. McIntosh, *Tourism Principles, Practices and Philosophies*, Grid Inc, 1972.

2 Doxey.

3 IBRD. (Leakage in the first round of expenditure).

Table 18. Total industrial output and output generated by tourist expenditure in the Barbados economy, 1968
($m)

Industrial sector	Total output	Output generated by tourist expenditure	% contribution
Sugar cane growing	30.3	0.23733	0.1
Other agriculture	25.3	1.31167	5:2
Sugar and molasses	36.6	0.19405	0.5
Other manufactures	79.6	8.70169	10.9
Quarrying	2.2	0.06518	0.3
Utilities	12.5	1.69663	13.6
Distribution	62.5	2.53472	4.1
Transport and communications	32.0	3.84352	12.0
Banking, Insurance and Real estate	31.4	2.06266	6.6
Construction	79.7	1.18690	1.5
Rents	20.2	0.64812	3:2
Hotels	25.4	25.40216	100.0
Other services	30.7	6.91108	22.5
Total	468.4	54.79571	11.6

Source: W. E. Armstrong et al. 'A Structural Analysis of the Barbados Economy' in *Social and Economic Studies*, Vol. 23, No. 4, December 1974, Table 1, p. 494 and Table 24, p. 517.

Investment and returns in tourism

The return on investment in tourism in most, if not all, cases tends to be overstated because of the improper accounting for investment in tourism and revenue generated from tourism. *Tourism-induced* investment could be defined as any investment which otherwise would not have been made, be less extensive or have less priority if there were no tourism or expected increases in tourist traffic. Under such a definition investment in tourism could include investment in hotel residential complexes, restaurants and infrastructural facilities, shops and night clubs. Such investment can be undertaken by both the private and public sector. It is

Table 19. Estimates of revenue from tourism in Barbados, Jamaica and St Vincent
(EC$m)

	1970	1971	1972	1973	1974
Barbados	63,500,000	66,000,000	119,900,000	136,400,000	156,600,000
Jamaica	175,120,000	199,760,000	237,380,000	254,760,000	271,260,000
St Vincent	6,000,000	7,000,000	8,000,000	9,000,000	...

difficult on a pure economic return basis to gauge the effectiveness of such expenditure. The revenue obtained would be an estimate of all the revenue generated by such investments. It is strongly felt by the author that, because of improper accounting for this investment, its contribution to the GDP is underestimated.[1]

Employment — present and future prospects

It is estimated that there is a one-to-one correspondence between the number of hotel rooms, the directly employed and the indirectly employed. The estimates for Jamaica and Barbados in Table 20 both made use of this rule of thumb. In Jamaica there are approximately 10,000 rooms. Hence it is assumed that there are 10,000 directly and 10,000 indirectly employed, giving an estimate in the range of 20,000. In the case of the directly employed these figures in some cases are based on an actual physical count. In the case of the indirectly employed this is an estimate for which no empirical evidence has been seen. If the linkages in the various economies have different strengths and if there is a significant difference in the production structure of the LDCs as opposed to the MDCs, it is very questionable whether each dollar of tourism expenditure admitted to have distinct income-generating effects will have the same induced employment effects. The ratio of rooms to the number of people directly employed should in fact differ from country to country, for it is dependent on the distribution mix of hotel type. For small hotels and residential complexes it is estimated that the ratio is in the range of 0.5 employees per room.

Table 20. Contribution of tourism to employment in Jamaica and Barbados

	Jamaica	Barbados
Employment in tourism	20,300	9,000
Labour force	810,000	90,200
Employment in tourism as % of labour force	2.5	10.0
Employed labour force	637,000	82,400
Employment in tourism as % of employed labour force	3.2	10.9

Sources: For Jamaica, *Economic and Social Survey*, 1973, and Shankland Cox, *Tourism Supply in the Caribbean*; for Barbados, *Central Bank Report*.

Despite the high level of under-employment and redundancy through seasonality, tourism makes a significant contribution to increasing employment. In most cases workers employed are non-skilled and previously non-employed and their marginal productivity in alternative

1 See Appendix.

endeavours is either negligible or zero. This is in the context of unemployment running at over 20% in most of the countries.

Future prospects

If there is a one-to-one correspondence between hotel rooms and employees and also a one-to-one correspondence between the directly employed in tourism and those indirectly employed, then there is a very high positive correlation between hotel rooms constructed, and the level of direct and indirect employment.

Earlier, in the analysis of hotel construction, it was recommended that owing to excess capacity in all the CARICOM islands except Montserrat, hotel building should be placed under stringent scrutiny and control. The high growth rate required to achieve adequate occupancy makes it inconceivable that the industry will show significant if any profitability within five years or more, even if no further hotel construction is assumed.

There should be little or no completed hotel construction in any of the Caribbean countries within the next five years[1], unless there is a high probability of achieving the annual growth rates required to achieve occupancy significantly higher then break-even. Hence in the foreseeable future hotel development will make an insignificant contribution to fixed capital investment and to capital formation, and also to additional employment. The rate of absorption of the labour force will be directly dependent on the rate of attrition and turnover of those now employed. This rate is low, owing to the low age of present workers and the tendency to work to past retiring age.

This will create many problems in the industry which is already suffering from the fact that hotel development was not conceived within a framework of co-ordinated long-range planning. There has been an expression of concern (regionally) for trained personnel to take up the positions of expatriates and to assume duties at the higher levels in present and new hotels. Because of the seasonality and apparent instability of the industry (not discounting the fact that the top hierarchy of the organisation is foreign-dominated) the industry has not attracted as many talented locals as it should. The industry consequently has to create the environment where nationals perceive a future in hotel training and are induced to assume training of their own volition or take advantage of the training provided by government (if any). Clearly the immediate problem is to avoid or deal with the frustrations that will arise when a number of naionals who are now pursuing training at the various levels find difficulty in obtaining employment. The problem is complicated by the time lag between the decisions induced by a particular set of considerations and the implementation of such decisions.

---

1 Except Dominica, Trinidad and Montserrat.

Future strategy

Clearly the Caribbean has inherited a legacy of incoherent and unco-ordinated tourism planning strategies; incoherent in the sense that such strategies do not cohere with what ought to be national or regional objectives. There seems little that could be done significantly to alter the distribution pattern of profits in the hotel sector within the next five years. However, what could be done in this period is to ensure that the pattern is not perpetuated. Properly conceived plans and strategies to ensure these plans are achieved, that projects are properly timed, interlinked and co-ordinated are necessary. The unlikelihood of the tourism sector generating significant additional employment in the next five years should impress upon the decision-makers the urgency of developing and strengthening linkages. Such plans should be bolstered by a change in the pattern of consumption expenditure from consumer durables and imported items. There is also a need for improvement in the basic infrastructural facilities in most, if not all, of the LDCs.

Appendix

Indicators of the contribution of the tourism sector in selected Caribbean economies

	Antigua	Barbados	Jamaica
Population	65,000 (1970)	243,741 (1971)	1,935,000 (1972)
Tourist arrivals	73,238 (1971)	310,435 (1971)	475,256 (1972)
GDP at factor cost	EC$ 57.7m (1971)	EC$455.6m (1972)	J$ 1093.5m (1971)
Contribution of tourism to GDP, 1971 (%)	40-50	20	6
Labour force	35,000[1] (1970)	90,200 (1970)	800,000 (1973 April)
Employment in tourism	1,247[2]	9,000	20,300
Employment in tourism as % of labour force	4	10	2.5
Foreign exchange earnings from tourism and merchandise trade	$ 29.2m (1970)	$ 87.2m (1972)	$ 446.7m (1972)
Foreign exchange earnings from tourism	$ 15.6m (1970)	$ 45.0m (1972)	$ 85.8m (1972)
Tourism earnings as % of foreign exchange earnings from tourism and merchandise trade in years indicated above	53.4	51.6	19.2
Foreign-owned hotel rooms as % of total hotel rooms	...	64.0[3]	50[2]
Foreign ownership of hotels (by numbers)	...	42.0	27

1 Estimate.
2 World Bank estimate (1970).
3 Hotels only based on 1970-71 list published by Barbados Tourist Board.

Sources: B. Watson, in Supplementary Notes on Foreign Investment, IBRD *Caribbean Regional Study*, Volume VIa, National Planning Agency—Economic and Social Survey.

6. Housing in the Commonwealth Caribbean and the Experience of the CDC

Regional Controller (East Caribbean),
Commonwealth Development Corporation

CDC was established by an Act of the UK Parliament in 1948 as the Colonial Development Corporation to assist the economic development of the then dependent territories of the Commonwealth. The change of name to Commonwealth Development Corporation was effected in 1963 when Parliament also restored CDC's full powers of operation in all those countries which had achieved independence since 1948. CDC is empowered to undertake, either alone or in association with others, projects for the promotion or expansion of a wide range of economic enterprises including agriculture, forestry, fisheries, mining, factories, electricity and water undertakings, transport, housing, hotels, building, and engineering.

Within its wide terms of reference CDC has invested in the East Caribbean in a variety of projects. Many of these have had to make provision for housing for employees. However, such enterprises are dealt with in this paper only if their main activity is directed to housing.

Early experience with housing

Castries, St Lucia

In 1948 a fire destroyed over 24 acres of business and residential property in Castries, capital of St Lucia. Over 2,500 people were made homeless. The government turned to CDC for assistance and appointed the Corporation as agents and consulting engineers for the reconstruction project. The final cost of the contracts was £1.25m and resulted in the construction of government offices, law courts, post office, telephone exchange, government printing press, town hall, fire station, police station, library, warehouses, customs house, as well as residential housing comprising two-storey maisonettes and flats, four-storey flats, flats combined with shops and three-bedroom houses. The contracts were awarded in 1949 and completed in 1951. Unusually for CDC, although it managed this project, it did not provide any of the finance.

Building materials

Apart from the Castries reconstruction CDC's only other involvements in housing in the period up to 1960 were indirect. In the then British Guiana CDC acquired a timber enterprise in 1949 and expanded this to produce a variety of timber products, including a large proportion of the local demand for the traditional all-wood houses. In Trinidad CDC was associated in the establishment of a cement company to supply local and West Indian markets.

Post-1960 experience: general

The 1960s and 1970s to date have seen a growing involvement by CDC in housing in the East Caribbean. As a general rule the Corporation prefers to separate the development/construction function from mortgage finance operations. The two jobs require different management and technical skills. Also the type of finance required is different — construction aiming at a quick turnover of funds whereas mortgage finance, by definition, is a long-term investment. Moreover it is considered a good discipline for the mortgage institution which is, in a sense, the developer's customer, to be able to give an independent assessment of the value of the property being offered as a security. Although in practice the separation of functions has sometimes not been complete, it is convenient to review them separately.

CDC as a developer

CDC normally regards any housing development activity as essentially a 'seeding' operation and would hope that private developers would take over this function as soon as possible. In many countries, however, it has been found that the building industry is very poorly organised, consisting of under-capitalised, small concerns capable really only of the 'one-off' operation. In order to demonstrate what can be done to reduce selling prices by introducing estate-type development, CDC has entered this field in several countries in the East Caribbean — sometimes in partnership with others but frequently entirely on its own. In some cases what may be grandly called 'estate developments' have of necessity consisted of very modest numbers because of local limitations. The inhibiting factors in determining the size of any particular estate and indeed housing generally are scarcities — land, skilled labour, materials and market. In the smaller islands particularly, the governments have a difficult task deciding between the conflicting demands for land. On the one hand the necessity to boost food production and export earnings, which normally means increasing agricultural production, argues in favour of reserving land for farming, but political pressures from populations with an awakened appetite for a better standard of living call for additional areas to be set aside for residential purposes. Understandably, the solution has often been to allocate for housing land which is not suitable for agriculture, especially hilly areas. This has naturally increased the costs of development of infrastructure and even of the houses themselves. Skilled artisans and supervisors are not readily available. All too often those who are trained are tempted to move to more developed countries. Of course the provision of better housing is itself a factor in persuading skilled workers to remain in their home countries. Periodic shortages of building materials are a fact of life in the East Caribbean, especially in the smaller islands. One of the advantages of an estate development is that it can enable the contractor to place a bulk order for direct supply by the manufacturer rather than rely on the local agent. This can produce significant cost savings as well as ensuring that construction is not disrupted by shortages. These problems would no doubt be overcome, with varying degrees of success, provided a developer can rely on an adequate market for his finished products.

As so few people anywhere in the world can afford to pay cash for a house, the most effective way of supporting housing development is by the provision of adequate mortgage finance. It is in this aspect of housing that CDC has been most active in the East Caribbean.

CDC as mortgagee

It is possible to make a very reasoned case against an international organisation like CDC investing in mortgages. Housing is not a foreign exchange earner except to the very limited extent that expatriates remit funds home to purchase housing. Investment of sterling in housing loans therefore has a negative effect on the foreign currency budgets of the host countries when the loans have to be serviced. However, CDC found that it could not ignore the very real and justified demand for better housing by the lower- and middle-income groups in the East Caribbean and has set up a number of mortgage finance agencies. In no country has it been possible to establish an organisation directly comparable with UK building societies which lend only funds derived from savings. CDC has set up mortgage finance companies with a significant element of equity capital, supplemented by loan capital repayable normally on fixed terms. It would hope that normally such companies would either at the start or at an early stage attract government participation in both equity and loans. Thereafter the next stage in evolution would be to accept deposits from individuals and/or the private enterprise sector. The increasing proportion of local funds would help to dilute the foreign capital and therefore reduce the risk of currency realignments adversely affecting the mortgage institutions.

The general pattern of mortgage finance companies established by CDC in the East Caribbean is one of government support from the start, at least to the extent of tax concessions. The host governments have normally felt justified in granting total tax exemption in exchange for undertakings by the mortgage finance company to operate within certain parameters — especially on the maximum size of loan and the maximum rate of interest charged. The combined effect is to make mortgage loans available to the lower- and middle-income groups. The higher-income groups have often been reasonably well catered for by established institutions — the commercial banks and insurance companies.

In this pioneering activity CDC has encountered a number of problems. In the absence of a pool of persons trained in mortgage lending, CDC has inevitably had to train its own administrators and was not always fortunate enough to select the right personnel for training. Where staff have been inadequate, loans have been granted to people who do not earn enough to be able to repay the loans or on properties which are not adequate security for the loans. When the lending institutions reluctantly decide that they have to recover loans in default by proceeding against the properties they have often found that the legal machinery is imperfect — either in effecting the initial security or in giving adequate remedies. These problems have exercised the minds of those in CDC concerned with the mortgage finance companies and, especialy in the last two years, a comprehensive review of all procedures has been carried out. New operating manuals have been prepared and introduced. It is confidently expected that the companies will be able to play an increasing role in meeting the housing needs of the various countries, particularly in those cases where the government is or will become an active partner.

Review by country

Barbados

1968 was the year in which CDC dramatically increased its involvement in housing in the East Caribbean and Barbados was no exception. In that year two development companies were established — East Caribbean Housing Ltd, a 100% subsidiary based in Barbados but not confined to activities in that country, and Rock Dundo Development Co Ltd, a 50/50 partnership with Northern Foods Ltd, of Hull, which was established to develop a specific estate in Barbados. Also in 1968 CDC formed the Barbados Mortgage Finance Co Ltd in which the Barbados government joined as minority shareholder. The government has also since provided or secured substantial loan capital.

The Rock Dundo Development Co Ltd completed its programme in 1972, having built 127 houses all of which have been sold. The company will now be wound up. East Caribbean Housing Ltd has also completed its construction programme, that for Barbados consisting of 334 houses.

Together these two development companies provided the bulk of the business for the mortgage finance company which now has 635 active mortgage accounts with a total outstanding of Bds$14m (equivalent to £3.5m). Unfortunately the government National Housing Corporation has not been able to deliver as many houses as was planned and therefore lending has fallen behind target.

Dominica

East Caribbean Housing Ltd developed two modest estates — one near Roseau and the other on land released by another CDC project — the Melville Hall agricultural estate. The Dominica Mortgage Finance Company Ltd was formed in 1968. Unfortunately legal problems have inhibited this company's development and it has only 309 active mortgage accounts, with an outstanding debt of EC$5m (equivalent to £1m).

Guyana

As already stated, CDC was involved at a very early stage with the production of timber through what is now Guyana Timbers Ltd. In 1959 the company began production of prefabricated houses for sale throughout the West Indies. By 1967 this side of the business had been greatly extended and it was hoped that a large number of such houses would be sold to a scheme in Georgetown which was to have been financed by USAID. Unfortunately the contractor went into liquidation before the project got under way. Nevertheless GTL was ready to supply houses for export and to the Guyana Housing & Development Co Ltd, a 100% CDC subsidiary formed in 1967 to develop land acquired from the government in Georgetown and New Amsterdam. To complete the vertical development another 100% subsidiary, the Guyana Mortgage Finance Co Ltd, was established in 1968 to lend to the buyers of the GTL houses built on GHDC-developed plots. Between them these companies have built and/or financed some 2,000 houses. The total outstanding on some 1,900 mortgage accounts is G$19.7m (£3.7m). In addition to building individual houses for sale, GHDC has built a very popular block of rental apartments and a shopping complex in its main housing estate at South Ruimveldt.

In an attempt to ease some of the production bottlenecks CDC invested in 1970 in a company which proposed to expand its stone-quarrying business into ready-mixed cement and cement blocks. Regrettably the concept was too revolutionary for the local construction industry and the venture failed.

Unfortunately the Guyana government chose not to join CDC in partnership in its various housing-related companies. In 1972 it acquired Guyana Timbers Ltd, and subsequently set up its own Housing Corporation and Mortgage Finance Bank which now operate to a certain extent in competition with their counterparts in the CDC group. CDC is not satisfied with this situation and the future of its housing activities in Guyana is therefore under review.

St Lucia

Reference has already been made to the early association of CDC with the rebuilding of Castries in 1949-51. In 1967 CDC lent £210,000 to the Urban Development Corporation towards the cost of site works and reclamation of 58 acres in Castries which were developed for residential purposes.

In the following year, 1968, CDC set up a wholly-owned subsidiary, the St Lucia Mortgage Finance Company Ltd, which lent to persons buying houses from the Urban Development Corporation and to individuals building their own houses. East Caribbean Housing Ltd also developed modest estates in St Lucia using prefabricated houses from Guyana, and these also were financed by the mortgage finance company. The company currently has 560 active mortgage accounts with a total of EC$9.9m (£2.1m) outstanding.

These developments were aimed at the lower- and middle-income groups of St Lucians. CDC has also been involved in developments aimed at the more affluent, especially foreigners who are looking for holiday or retirement homes. These developments are taking place at the northern end of the island. In 1971 CDC agreed to lend £100,000 to the Cap Estate St Lucia Ltd to help the company develop 1,500 acres for residential purposes. Adjoining this estate is the Rodney Bay scheme in which CDC, the government, and Jamaican interests are partners and which CDC manages. This very imaginative venture has already created an attractive 75-acre salt-water yacht lagoon out of an unhealthy swamp, has joined historic Pigeon Island to the mainland by means of a causeway, and deepened the Rodney Bay waters. As a result of these activities the company has available some 500 acres which will be developed as an integrated tourist and residential complex with hotels, condominium apartments, houses, and a yacht marina. To support sales of the residential accommodation a new mortgage institution has been established which will devote its funds solely to this development.

St Vincent

The St Vincent Housing Finance Co Ltd was established in 1970 as a 100% subsidiary. Unusually this company, for special reasons, combined the roles of developer and mortgagee. A 42-house estate was built at Arnos Vale but generally housing development has been slow on this economically depressed island and the mortgage business has only reached the stage of 165 accounts with a total of EC$2.8m (£0.6m) owing. Because of its small size and a reluctance by government to agree to more realistic lending rates the company does not operate profitably.

Trinidad and Tobago

CDC's indirect involvement in housing in Trinidad dates back to 1951 when it was associated with the establishment of a cement industry. With the recent repayment of the loan to this company CDC is no longer an investor.

In 1961 CDC took a 50% shareholding in the Trinidad Mortgage Agency Ltd and agreed to lend up to £2m. The plans envisaged mortgages on 2,000 houses. In the event the project was a very slow starter. There were difficulties over the legislation, land titles, developers, and sales. Work stopped in 1963, by which time only 217 houses had been completed. The final total of mortgage loans was only 92.

In 1965 CDC tried again but this time in partnership with the government. The Trinidad and Tobago Mortgage Finance Co Ltd was formed, and CDC agreed to contribute £1m in equity and a further £1m in loans; government put up a total of £0.5m, half in equity, half in loans. CDC entered into a management agreement.

The new company aimed particularly at the lower- and middle-income groups and lent on houses built by the government National Housing Authority as well as approved private developers. It took over management of the small portfolio of mortgages built up by the Trinidad Mortgage Agency.

In the first few years the company was held back by a shortage of houses, but in 1969 nearly 500 loans were granted. Unhappily this trend has been reversed and recently lending has again been depressed.

In 1969 CDC established an unincorporated mortgage fund to make loans to purchasers of houses in the Montrose Neighbourhood Development scheme in central Trinidad. By 1972 the fund was fully drawn by 79 borrowers and the accounts are also managed by the mortgage finance company.

The total number of mortgage accounts administered by the company is just under 2,000 and the total outstanding is TT$23m (£4.8m).

CDC renegotiated its relationship with its partner and in terms of an agreement signed in 1974 control of the mortgage finance company will pass to government in 1976.

Conclusion

Has it all been worthwhile?

If CDC were a private commercial concern the answer would have to be 'no'. The various housing development and mortgage finance companies have absorbed a great deal of time of all levels of executive staff both in the East Caribbean and in the London head office, and the net returns on the capital invested have been marginal.

However, in fulfilling CDC's development function the effort has produced results. Several thousand families, tens of thousands of individuals, have been enabled to acquire their own homes. Many of these homes started off as very basic units by the standards of a developed country but they represent a substantial improvement on their previous housing for most of the people. Anyone who visits one of the estates which CDC has created or helped to create in the East Caribbean will be struck by the real pride being shown in these homes; gardens have been lovingly established, and many of the houses have been extended or modified to express the individuality of the owner. Such a visitor must conclude that the effort was worthwhile.

7. Arguments for Aiding a Programme of Divestment

M. L. O. Faber
Overseas Development Group,
University of East Anglia

> 'Clearly, political independence and national sovereignty are inconsistent with a situation in which the "commanding heights" of the economy are foreign-owned and controlled . . . it must be at the very least a long range objective to bring these sectors of the economy under local ownership of one sort or another' (p. 104). 'The question is not whether to use foreign capital in development planning. Rather the question is how to bring foreign capital into harmony with national aspirations' (p. 106). 'Our great problem is to find the proper balance and mix between foreign capital already in Jamaica, the new capital that we need and the institutions of control and systems of ownership which can ensure that economic development is consistent with national objectives (p. 84).[1]

If foreign investment is to be successful, it must be welcome. But if foreign investors are to be welcomed, and to *remain* welcome, they will increasingly need to show not only the terms upon which they intend to come in and operate, but also the time and the terms upon which they will be prepared to pass over control and go. What is being proposed in this paper is that the acts of deliberate political decolonisation that occurred in the quarter century following 1945 should now be succeeded by a period when actions would be taken deliberately to diminish those economic influences that are widely regarded in the Commonwealth Caribbean as constituting the most objectionable manifestations of neo-colonialism. Because initiative in this area, at least from the side of the investing countries, is novel, it is likely to be delayed. But if it is too long delayed, the period during which a deliberate receding of neo-colonial influences could be implemented through negotiation will pass, and will almost certainly be succeeded by a period when such mutually advantageous solutions will no longer be possible.

It is not mainly because some of the consequences of some investments are considered objectionable that corrective mechanisms need to be

1 Michael Manley, 'The Restructuring of a Post-Colonial Economy,' in *The Politics of Change—A Jamaican Testament*, London, Andre Deutsch, 1974.

introduced. This is in itself a reason, but it is not the main one. More important reasons are:

(a) that control over its most important economic and industrial decisions from within a country is in itself an essential element of development and political independence;

(b) that while foreign investments will bring about development of one kind, they may also render impossible social and economic developments of other kinds far more vital to the country in the longer run[1].

The Hirschman proposal

At the Columbia Conference on International Economic Development held at Williamsburg, Virginia, in February 1970, Albert Hirschman, whose heresies have a habit of turning later into dogma, delivered a paper entitled 'How to Divest in Latin America, and Why'[2]. In it he mentioned that he had proposed, as early as 1961, (and with 'total lack of success') to the International Finance Corporation that it should devote a portion of its resources to acquiring foreign-owned assets in developing countries, and holding them until such time as they could be placed with local investors. Later Dr Raul Prebisch suggested that an agency should be established within the Inter-American Development Bank for this purpose. I mention this to show that the ideas propounded here are not, in essence, either original or new. They are, as ideas go, in lusty adolescence though not yet confirmed by the maturity of practice.

Disinvestments by foreign enterprises do of course occur — through deliberate running down or sale of assets, or through forced sales, bankruptcies, war-time confiscations, expropriations or nationalisations of various degrees. But what has been lacking has been any deliberate, pre-planned programme of divestments — negotiated, financed and carried through. It is the sort of programme that could best be conducted, initially, in the laboratory of a limited region, between nations enjoying amicable relations, and during a period when no quarrel is being waged over any specific act of expropriation. The Caribbean is such a region, the present is such a period, Commonwealth ties provide an excellent context for amicable negotiations, and the Caribbean Development Bank is in many ways ideally placed to serve as the 'divestment corporation' (Hirschman's

---

1 For reasons why plantation agriculture may have particularly adverse effects upon local social and economic advancement see G. L. Bleckford's 'The Economics of Agricultural Resource Use and Development in Plantation Economies' in *Social and Economic Studies*, Vol. 18, 1969.

2 Published as *Essays in International Finance*, No. 76, by the International Finance Section, Princeton University; and in Barbara Ward, Lenore D'Anjou and J. D. Runnals (eds), *The Widening Gap—Development in the 1970s*, Columbia University Press, 1971.

name) to which our disengaging investors would progressively transfer their assets.

Ways and means

How, in outline, might such an arrangement operate? And what would be the advantages of it to the parties involved?

We must start by distinguishing the problems that arise from existing investments from those that would arise in connection with new investments. How, it will be asked, is consideration to be paid for assets that will often be of enormous value in relation to the resources available to the government of the host country? No single source of finance could, or should, be looked for. The aim should rather be to look for a combination of payments, or streams of future payments, that would together constitute a fair replacement for the legal ownership and some part of the control over the assets which are being divested. Notice that only 'some part of the control' is to be relinquished and therefore compensated for. Foreign investors in existing circumstances do not exercise complete control over the operation of their assets, be they mines, plantations, factories, or hotels. All are subject to general regulations imposed by the host government, and many are likely to be subject to special regulations and controls as well. So it is not complete control in that literal sense that is being surrendered. It will also be useful to consider arrangements whereby some control over some aspects of the firm's operations may continue to be exercised, through mutual agreement, even after majority ownership of the assets has been transferred. Such partial control might itself be exercised partly through management contracts or other forms of agreement and partly through the influence of a residual equity holding that might be in the region of, say, 10% to 25%.

Notice too that any reduction in the risk associated with the receipt of future remittances will have the effect of reducing also the accumulated amount which it will be appropriate to pay. This is a factor which should make it easier to arrive at compensating settlements that would be agreeable to both sides. If we assume that the disinvestment corporation, as agent for the host governments, will discount the risk element in future dividend receipts at a lower rate than the vulnerable foreign investor, then the acquisition by the investor of a secure stream of compensatory payments, relatively heavy in the early years but terminating rapidly in exchange for his giving up an indefinite stream of anticipated future dividends, can theoretically leave both parties to the transaction in a preferred position. The problem, in a sense, becomes one of providing the divestment corporation with bridging finance.

Let us suppose, for an example, that one country in the Commonwealth Caribbean found one specific foreign investment particularly objectionable, and was eager that ownership and control of the company should be seen to pass into Caribbean hands. Let us suppose too, for the moment, that a price and form of payment acceptable to all parties involved had been negotiated. Now let us ask what the ingredients of the purchase price might be, and how they would be financed.

The purchase price might be composed of some or all of the following components:

a cash component to be paid by the divestment corporation;

a cash component to be contributed by the host government, possibly through the divestment corporation;

divestment corporation bonds or loan stock, the payments schedules of which would need to be met by the earnings from all shareholdings taken over;

share purchases made either directly or through the divestment corporation by pension funds, insurance companies, development corporations and/or individuals in the host country;

payment at an agreed valuation for any purchasing and marketing contracts, royalty and fee obligations, management and consultancy agreements that might be negotiated with the divestor on behalf of the newly independent local company[1].

Hirschman lists three other possible sources of finance:

the agency could 'sell, on the instalment plan, a substantial portion and perhaps a majority, of the equity of the erstwhile foreign firms to white- and blue-collar workers, with first choice being given to those employed in such firms';

'since the presence in a country of foreign interests that are felt as irritants poses a danger for the prosperity and, indeed, the life of *all* foreign firms . . . a contribution from all corporations with foreign assets can be justified';

'the agency may well be the ideal beneficiary of the much discussed "link" between the new monetary reserves created as a result of the Agreement (Special Drawing Rights) and the developing countries. The principal objection against any such link has been that the reserves created should not become a mechanism for effecting permanent transfers of real resources from one set of countries to another. This objection would be largely met if the industrial countries used part of their allocation of SDRs for the subscription of capital or bond issues of the Divestment Corporation'.

In many instances comparable arrangements, quite possibly incorporating other institutions, might be required to take care of the long-term debt

1 Some indication of the potential value of such contracts is given by the compensation which the government of Zambia agreed to pay, amounting to 54m kwacha (about £35m), following the termination of its management and sales contracts with Zambian Anglo American and Roan Selection Trust. The government of Zaire's payment of compensation for its nationalisation of the majority shareholding in its copper mines was also made largely by means of remunerative management contracts.

obligations of the divested company, if the lenders were entitled to call in their loans following any transfer of majority ownership or control. These could undeniably cause some difficulty, although not of a kind that major lending institutions are unfamiliar with. There is the compensating point, however, that the larger the debt element, the less would be the sum required to pay for the equity.

It is not suggested that the components outlined above should always be called upon, or that other devices should not be used. An essential ingredient of any programme of this kind would have to be precisely that flexibility for which the corporate structure is famous, and which has enabled the larger companies to prosper through so many vicissitudes. It is worth remembering that a hundred years ago, at the time of the Scramble for Africa, European governments believed that unless they were able to secure colonies under their own control, their manufacturers would be unable to gain either access to that continent's raw materials or outlets in its markets. What is needed now is a release from similar beliefs and similar institutional arrangements with regard to the ownership and control by Western-based companies of their more powerful overseas subsidiaries.

Many objections can be raised against the whole concept of divestment and against the manner in which it is proposed that relinquished assets should be paid for. One school of thought will argue that the assets should certainly be taken over, but that they should not be paid for at all. There is an established theory of expropriation, and assorted guidelines for practical action. It is not the purpose of this paper to deny that there will be circumstances which make expropriation or unilateral nationalisation the most advantageous course for a host government to pursue in its own economic interest. These proposals relate to a different and possibly more common set of circumstances — when the costs of expropriation and its consequences are considered to be greater than those of an agreed and assisted purchase of majority ownership and control.

As to the proposed components of compensation, the first and most obvious difficulty is that no indication is given as to where the divestment corporation itself will obtain its funds. The initial capital would have to come without doubt from aid funds, some of it from international institutions and some, for particular purchases, from the aid programme of the countries where the company being bought out was resident. International institutions have not yet shown much enthusiasm for advancing funds for the purpose of buying out foreign investors. But they may begin to do so when they perceive (as Hirschman has argued) that the existence of powerful foreign business interests in developing economies frequently serves to distort national economic decision-making by governments and may, albeit unintentionally, act in a way that stunts the growth of local business and impedes the development of indigenous forms of productive organisation. It may likewise seem curious to suggest that the UK should provide the Caribbean Development Bank with funds to buy out a British company in, say, Jamaica — although businessmen have been known to advance money to their workers to enable them to buy out the business that they work in. But is it so curious? Aid in this form would have no immediate adverse balance of payments effect, while even the long-term effect could be comparatively slight, and it could produce positive diplomatic advantages[1].

It is to be hoped therefore that it would be incremental to existing aid budgets, both internationally and nationally — but even if this were not the case, there might still be sound grounds for replacing some capital aid projects with funds to finance divestment. A leading requirement in most Commonwealth Caribbean countries — even more urgent than new infrastructural projects — is investments that will produce more revenue for government and net additions to foreign exchange. Investment in divestment, always provided that the localised assets are efficiently run, would produce both.

An argument that will certainly be raised is that aid funds ought to go to finance the implementation of new developments, not simply a transfer in ownership of existing assets. In support of traditional projects it will be urged that they have two beneficial effects — one through employment- and income-generation while the project is being constructed, the other through the operation of the project when it is completed. It is certainly not the purpose of this paper to argue against well selected projects of this kind, and to the extent that funds for divestment are incremental to existing aid finance, the two need not

1 The final report of the Reddaway Study on 'Effect of UK Direct Investment Overseas' (Department of Applied Economics Occasional Papers: No. 15, University of Cambridge) includes a section (pp. 244-9) and an appendix (pp. 382-7) on the 'Effects of Disinvestment'. The conclusion arrived at is that on a broad view 'the income from the direct investment overseas in the form of profits was probably greater than even a generous estimate of the income from the alternative financial assets, and the inclusion of capital appreciation in the picture would enlarge the difference. Over and above that, disinvesting would have led to some loss to the UK balance of payments in the shape of a lower demand for exports of goods and services.' However, disinvestment in plantations was found to be a special case; '. . . ignoring capital appreciation, the net continuing effect on the UK balance of payments will be a loss of approximately £2½ per annum per £100 worth of disinvestment in the case of rubber, and approximately zero in the case of tea. If capital appreciation is included, the loss in the case of rubber would possibly be reduced to zero, while there might be a *gain* in the case of tea possibly amounting to rather over £1.' What happened to many of the rubber and tea plantations in Asia ten to twenty years ago may well be repeated in less than ten to twenty years from now in respect of sugar and banana interests in the Caribbean. More to the point, however, is the observation that agreed disinvestment arrangements could well lead to net effects upon the UK balance of payments *more* favourable than those quoted below.

be regarded as in competition. But even where there does have to be some trade-off, it is by no means clear *a priori* that the benefits the host country is in a position to receive by assuming ownership and control of an important segment of its own industry will necessarily be less than the benefits that would accrue from the most marginal investment of the same cost in its social or economic infrastructure. It would at the very least be interesting to see what recipient governments would choose to do if they were offered freedom of choice in this matter.

Then there is the question of efficiency. If divestment is to operate successfully, the firms whose assets are to be transferred will have to be efficiently selected, for there will certainly be run-down or loss-making foreign industries that vigorously will promote their own candidature for inclusion in the scheme. The whole business of the transfer and its financing will have to be efficiently negotiated, and the businesses, once they have been transferred, will have to be efficiently run. In ensuring such efficiencies the role of an agency such as the CDB will be crucial. Assuming that it adopts the role of divestment corporation, it will be taking on some of the functions of a regional merchant bank. But in all aspects of this new role — in selection, in negotiation, and in supervising operations — it will need to be in a position to make use of expert assistance.

Firms whose operations in the Caribbean constitute part of a vertically integrated industry with transnational units may appear to have special problems. The efficiency and profitability of their operations elsewhere around the world may be reliant upon regular supplies of primary products (bauxite, oil, bananas, sugar) from their Caribbean components. Loss of ownership of these components may thus appear to involve a potential cost far beyond any compensation that could be negotiated based upon the value or earnings power of the assets. Quite so. But it is precisely because the transnational nature of these companies gives rise to a potential conflict of interests in decision-making between what is best for the multinational corporation on a world basis and what is best for an individual economy within which it is a major force, that the host gevernments want more control.[1] One of the features of whatever starts to emerge as the New International Economic Order is certain to be more vigorous — and more institutionalised — exercise by developing country governments of the rights of ownership (including production targets and price setting) over their natural resources. The Jamaican government's imposition of production taxes on bauxite and

1 For possible conflicts between the objectives of multinational corporations and the ideal of Caribbean integration, see 'Corporate vs Caribbean Integration' by N. Girvan and O. Jefferson, in *New World Quarterly*, Vol. 4, No. 2, 1968.

the Icelandic government's assertion of a 200-mile fishing limit within which they claim the right to determine the size of catches are part of the same trend. The institutional model that is being proposed is one in which the power of the MNC to make local decisions within the LDC (a power which is already severely circumscribed) through the assertion of the rights of formal ownership and control will be replaced by a wide set of contractual arrangements. Such enforced changes may appear drastic in anticipation to the boards of the major companies concerned, just as similar divestment changes enforced by the US Anti-Trust Legislation must have seemed to many American corporations, but we can be confident that the companies will adapt to the new system, just as the major oil companies have adapted to loss of formal ownership of a major proportion of their fields of supply.[1] The fact is that the new owners of the assets will still need to run them efficiently and will still need to sell their output and will in most cases find it easiest, cheapest, and most efficient to sell to the former owners for onward sale into established markets. But the new owner will be in a position to negotiate (instead of being obliged to accept) production levels, prices, investment in expansion and, where appropriate, choice of techniques.

An interesting parallel (although not one which necessarily involves a change of ownership) exists in the proposal being considered by the industry committee of the Labour Party's national executive committee for an 'inward-investment board' which would monitor new and existing foreign investment in the United Kingdom. There is a parallel also, although a more distant one, to be found in proposals designed to make companies more responsible to the communities in which they operate.

New ventures

The discussion so far has concerned itself with the divestment of existing assets by foreign companies operating in the Caribbean. Turning to the problem of creating new assets and running new enterprises, we are likely to find the situation less fraught with entrenched attitudes and entrenched interests. The phenomenon of the 'joint venture' between host government and incoming investor is by now well established.

What is being suggested here is that, within the format of the joint venture, institutional facilities and funds should be made available to enable interests in the Caribbean to have a majority holding in the joint venture either from the outset or, what may often be more sensible, after a predetermined span of operations. The 'span of opera-

1 The desire of the Caribbean countries to obtain and exercise majority control of the companies mining their most valuable natural resource should be easily understood, and sympathetically supported, by a government which has set up its own British National Oil Corporation for precisely that purpose.

tions' need not be defined as a specific period of time. It could be after a certain production level is reached, or when all the external loans have been repaid, or after accumulated receipts by the investor have exceeded a certain multiple of his original investment, or after the discount rate required to equate all the investor's payments and all his receipts exceeds a certain figure, or a combination of some or all of these.

The problem is, therefore, not likely to be one of principle, but one of finance. After all, Western enterprises compete for the privilege of establishing factories and mines in Communist bloc countries, provide the patents, train the personnel, and procure a large part of the finance without expecting to hold any part of the ownership or to exercise control. It is really only a question of being prepared to do for the Caribbean countries what is already being done for Communist countries.

Nor can it be a question of the overall supply of finance for such new investments — for there is no reason why the total financing requirements for a new mine, plantation, or factory in which the contributing interest was held by the CDB should be any different from what it would be if the controlling interest were held by Reynolds, Bookers, or Lever Bros. Neither the total supply of international finance, nor the total financing requirement is affected by the issue of ownership. The problem is one of channelling — of making available to the CDB (or to whatever institution is to play this role) the funds that would otherwise be required by and available to Reynolds, Bookers or Lever Bros.

Seen in this way, the financing issue can be broken down into several constituent problems:

who will take the initiative in raising the money?
who will supply the money?
how will the servicing of the investment be assured?

Let us suppose that the enterprise to be started was a major mining enterprise.[1] Once the ore-body itself has been discovered, explored, and full information about it developed, there would be four types of entities that could be expected to be keen to get it into operation:

(a) the government of the country where the deposit was located;
(b) the consortium of contractors which would have the work of constructing the mine, including the suppliers of equipment;
(c) the company which would be responsible for operating the mine;
(d) the customers for the mine's products;

The host government, the contractors, and the operating company will all be in a position to raise finance from sources largely independent of each other, but probably it will need to be the customers —

1 This might be expected to require a total financing of upwards of £150m.

the importing countries of the future mine's products — who will increasingly be called upon to play the major role in raising the finance which will be required to make production possible. We know already that when demand for a primary product, the production of which cannot be expanded rapidly, exceeds the available supply, prices can rise extremely rapidly. Importers of such products, considered collectively, have therefore a triple motive for investing in the expansion of supply. The investment itself should yield a satisfactory return. More important than that, the investment will help to assure continuity of supply and will also help to keep down the price. It should not be inferred from this that the actual firms who will buy the ore will be the entities to supply the major part of the required finance. It would be more realistic to view this matter in a wider context. In a world where traditional-type mining enterprises may no longer be able to go to their traditional sources to raise finance for the type of mine which the mining enterprise itself would expect to *own* as well as operate, the governments of those countries which need to import primary commodities will surely come to realise that it is in their own interests, as customers, to make available the required finance through international lending agencies for the only kinds of productive organisation that the host government countries are willing to allow.

There remains the problem of servicing the investment. Taking the whole group of new enterprises collectively, this will be a matter mainly of ensuring efficient and competitive operation, rather than of foreign exchange scarcity. For the type of enterprise we are discussing, where a product is produced and sold, it should be true (provided a competent project appraisal has been carried out) that the sale of the product will either earn or save substantially more foreign exchange than is required to service the external investment that made production possible.

Here again the role of an organisation such as the CDB will be vital. For such an agency will be required to ensure both that only projects whose foreign exchange earnings/savings exceed their debt servicing schedules are financed by foreign debt, and that management is selected and can operate so as to realise these earnings.

Summary

Ten distinct advantages are claimed for the processes of divestment and self-extinguishing new investment advocated here:

(a) greater economic independence, in the form of a transfer of the power to take major industrial decisions to within the region, is itself an important form of development, and should be welcomed by all in favour of development; the more so since it is now recognised that other forms of social and political development will be atrophied by a deficient economic control;

(b) transfer of the ownership of assets constitutes one part of the progress towards a New International Economic Order. An acceptance by the foreign investor of a change from claiming the rights implicit in ownership to accepting the mutual obligations made explicit in a contract is one manifestation of 'receding neo-colonialism'. Developing countries' industries, as they become increasingly 'regionalised', will also want to satisfy themselves that they are increasingly able to obtain a full arms-length price for what they sell and to go to the cheapest international sources for what they buy;

(c) enforced localisation of prominent foreign-owned assets in the Caribbean is going to happen at some stage anyway. Once this fact is recognised, it becomes advantageous to the governments of both investing and recipient countries to start planning together how best it should happen;

(d) a planned divestment will remove in advance the causes of disputes in which governments would be certain to become involved;

(e) by providing a relatively painless method for removing the most noxious of foreign investments, the lot and security of the remaining investments would be much improved;

(f) we all of us welcome guests to our house more warmly if we know in advance when they are planning to leave. Hence, paradoxically, by making pre-provision for the orderly demise of existing investments and the self-demise of new ones, future foreign investments will be made more welcome, and the flow of approved investments may actually increase;

(g) acquisitions of profitable enterprises, provided continuity of efficient management is assured, will lead to a sustained increase in local revenues, a most desirable contrast to the sort of traditional capital aid projects which call for sustained increases in recurrent government expenditure;

(h) imaginatively designed, the processes described could provide a mechanism for promoting and facilitating social change within Caribbean countries, through new forms of ownership and worker participation;

(i) by localising management and liberating it from evident foreign control, the influence upon government of local personnel experienced in senior management would very much increase, thus improving the quality of economic policy making;

(j) 'the solution lies in increasing economic independence from the rich countries matched by an increasing interdependence with other developing countries'.[1] A regional institution such as the Caribbean Development Bank acting as 'divestment corporation',

1 The Haslemere Group, *Bananas—a Study of the Crisis in the Jamaican Banana Industry*.

and also acting as a merchant bank promoting and holding investments in countries throughout the region, would develop authority and expertise in the negotiation of agreements and in the overseeing of the efficient operation of those companies in which it held an interest. Indirectly, indeed, every country within the Caribbean Common Market would have an interest in the efficiency of all the major industrial enterprises within the region. Although this state of affairs would lead to difficulties, it should also serve to emphasise an important fact of modern life. Namely, that although it has proved possible for the countries of the Commonwealth Caribbean to achieve political independence piecemeal, economic independence will prove possible only if they act together.[1]

1 In a speech delivered at Montego Bay in July 1975 the Commonwealth Secretary General, Mr Shridath Ramphal, drew attention to three factors that are of relevance. He observed that it was 'inevitable that the international economic issue will become increasingly politicised'. He regretted the 'omissions from our catalogue of successes' of any common polcy on foreign investment or on regional integration industry. And he asked 'if a way must be found between the need of the smaller islands for a helping hand . . . and their fear of dominion from whatever quarter, why cannot we explore the potential of CARICOM itself to provide that collective supplement to self-determination?'

Appendix: List of Participants

Earle C. Baccus: Engineer, Business Promoters & Consultants Ltd, Trinidad.

Lloyd Best: Economist, University of the West Indies, and Secretary Tapia House Movement (opposition political party in Trinidad and Tobago).

Jilla Bond: British-North American Research Association.

Alan Boyd: Director of Caribbean Department of External Affairs, Ottawa, Canada.

G. R. E. Bullen: General Manager and Chief Executive, Caribbean Investment Corporation (CIC), St Lucia.

Colin Campbell: Director, Agricultural Board, Booker McConnell Limited, London.

Margaret Cornell: Overseas Development Institute.

Robert Cuthbert: Executive Director, Christian Action for the Development of the Caribbean, and Associate General Secretary, Caribbean Conference of Churches.

Frank Earwaker: Senior Economist, Country Programs Division, Latin America and Caribbean, World Bank, Washington DC.

R. H. G. Edmonds, CMG, MBE: Assistant Under Secretary for State supervising North American and Latin American Departments and the Caribbean, Foreign and Commonwealth Office, London.

M. L. O. Faber: Overseas Development Group, University of East Anglia.

L. J. Foster: Senior Agriculturalist to the Commonwealth Development Corporation.

George Goyder: Hon Secretary, British-North American Research Association.

Sir Bruce Greatbatch, KCVO, CMG, MBE: Director, British Development Division in the Caribbean.

Edith Hodgkinson: Conference rapporteur, Overseas Development Institute.

Sir Richard King, KCB, MC: Permanent Secretary, Ministry for Overseas Development.

Michael Laidler: Director General 8, Commission of the European Communities, Brussels.

John Leech: Responsible for European and international relations, including extensions of operations into non-Commonwealth countries, of the Commonwealth Development Corporation.

William H: Luers: Deputy Assistant Secretary for Inter American Affairs, Department of State, Washington DC.

Alister McIntyre: Secretary-General, CARICOM.

Norman S. MacLean: Chief of Division 7 (the Caribbean), Operations Department of the Inter-American Development Bank:

Dawn Penso: Economics Officer, Trade and Finance Division, Commonwealth Secretariat.

Timothy S: Prime: Director of Research and Statistics, Caribbean Tourism Research Centre, Trinidad.

Frank Rampersad: Director, Trade and Finance Division, Commonwealth Secretariat.

Sir Shridah Ramphal: Secretary General, Commonwealth Secretariat.

Keith Roache: Agricultural Advisor, Barclays Bank of Jamaica Limited.

Lt Col M. R. Robinson: Secretary, The West India Committee, London.

B. W. Ross: Chief Planning Officer, Caribbean Division, Canadian International Development Agency, Ottawa, Canada.

Lord Seebohm: Chairman of the conference; Chairman, Finance for Industry Limited; Director, Barclays Bank International Ltd; Chairman, Overseas Development Institute Council; Member, Executive Committee, British-North American Research Association:

Joan Tyrrell: Overseas Development Institute.

Simon Webley: Director, British-North American Research Association, and Director of Research, British-North American Committee.

George E. Williams: Executive Secretary, East Caribbean Common Market Secretariat, Antigua.

DeLisle Worrell: Director of Research, Central Bank of Barbados.

The British-North American Research Association

The British-North American Research Association (BNARA) was inaugurated in December 1969 as an independent, non-profitmaking organisation. Its primary purpose is to sponsor research into Anglo-North American economic relations in conjunction with the National Planning Association in Washington DC and the CD Howe Research Institute in Montreal. These three bodies sponsor the British-North American Committee (BNAC). The Association publishes studies of the BNAC which together with others are available from 6-14 Dean Farrar Street, London SW1.

The BNARA is a registered educational charity and is governed by an Executive Committee under the chairmanship of Sir David Barran. The Director is Simon Webley.

Some Current BNARA Publications

BN-17 *Higher Oil Prices: Worldwide Financial Implications*, a Policy Statement by the British-North American Committee and a Research Report by Sperry Lea, October 1975 (£1.50, $3.00)
BN-16 *Completing the GATT: Toward New International Rules to Govern Export Controls*, by C. Fred Bergsten, October 1974 (80p, $2.00)
BN-15 *Foreign Direct Investment in the United States: Opportunities and Impediments*, by Simon Webley, September 1974 (80p. $2.00)
BN-14 *The GATT Negotiations*, 1973-75: *A Guide to the Issues*, by Sidney Golt, April 1974 (£1, $2.50)
BN-13 *Problems of Economic Development in the Caribbean*, by David Powell, compiled from a study by Irene Hawkins, November 1973 (80p, $2.00).
BN-12 *The European Approach to Worker Management Relations*, by Innis Macbeath, October 1973 (£1, $2.50)
BN-11 *An International Grain Reserve Policy*, by Timothy Josling, July 1973 (40p, $1.00).
BN-10 *Man and His Environment*, by Harry G. Johnson, May 1973 (40p, $1.00)
BN-8 *Multinational Corporations in Developed Countries: A Review of Recent Research and Policy Thinking*, by Sperry Lea and Simon Webley, March 1973 (80p, $2.00)
BN-6 *Multinational Corporations and British Labour: A Review of Attitudes and Responses*, by John Gennard, January 1972 (80p, $2.00).

Netherton & Worth Ltd., London & Truro